Dear Dad
Wishing you all the best
on your 80th Birthday.

Lots of love

Peter, Jayne, Lydia and
x , xx , x♡x
♡

A Portrait of Lord's

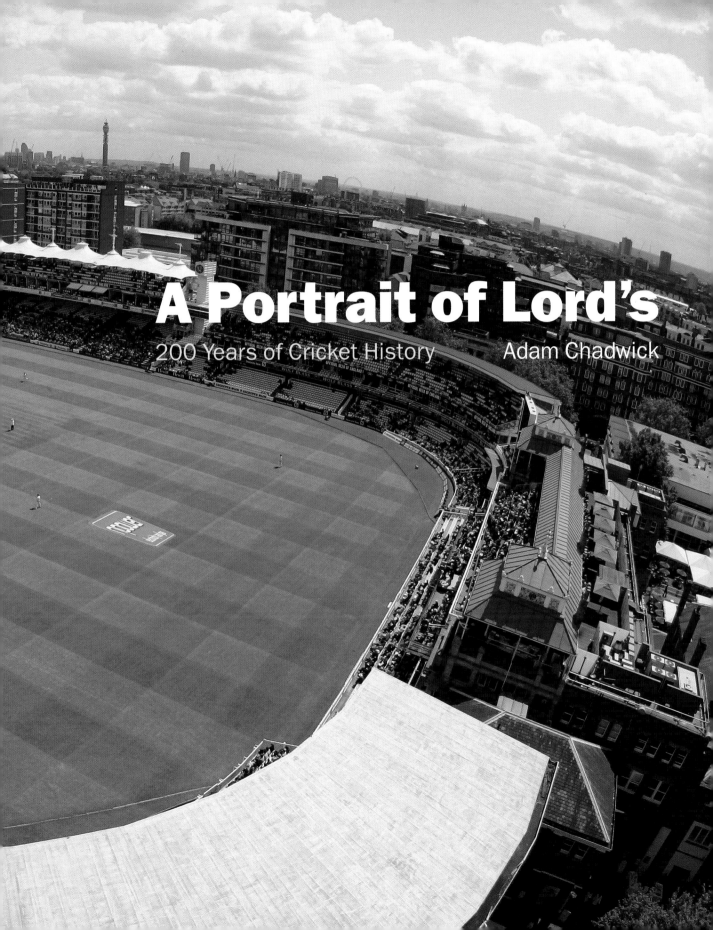

# A Portrait of Lord's

## 200 Years of Cricket History

### Adam Chadwick

First published in 2013 by
Scala Arts & Heritage Publishers Ltd
21 Queen Anne's Gate
London SW1H 9BU, UK
www.scalapublishers.com

In association with
Marylebone Cricket Club
Lord's Ground
London NW8 8QN, UK
www.lords.org

ISBN (hardback): 978-1-85759-829-2
ISBN (paperback): 978-1-85759-866-7

Edited by Oliver Craske
Designed by James Alexander
at JADE Design
Printed in Spain

10 9 8 7 6 5 4 3 2 1

Page 1: "The Bridge": the doorway
leading into the Lord's Pavilion from the
MCC Library. Closed on match days, it
is used by players escaping the public
eye at the end of play.

Pages 2–3: A panorama of Lord's from
high above the Warner Stand, with the
City of London beyond. Photographed
by Philip Brown in the morning session
of the fourth day of the First Test
against New Zealand, 18th May 2008.

Below: The 1966 World Cup Final
Football and the Ashes Urn. Lord's
hosted the launch of the *Our Sporting
Life* exhibition project in November
2008. Intent on highlighting the history
of sport in the UK, the Sports Heritage
Network, supported by the *Daily
Telegraph* and Arts Council, helped
deliver over 100 exhibitions nationwide
in the lead-up to the 2012 Olympics.

# Contents

# Foreword

It will always be special to me that the last shot I played in cricket was my favourite cover drive to go to a century and win a Test match at Lord's for England, with my mate Graham Thorpe at the other end against New Zealand. It really does not get any better than that and it is the main reason why I have never been tempted to pick up a cricket bat in anger ever since.

It was perfect, of course, because it was at Lord's. It would not have been quite the same, with respect, if it had been at Chelmsford or Derby, and I am proud that the bat with which I scored that century is now part of the Lord's collection which this book celebrates.

Lord's is still my favourite place to watch cricket now as a commentator. It remains a privilege that I am allowed to step out onto that hallowed turf before a day's play and you really can't beat the atmosphere, that unique buzz, that you get at the home of cricket.

It was not like that at first. When I started playing at Lord's as a young batsman I was a bit anti-establishment and thought of Lord's as an unfriendly place, somewhere where you would run into all sorts of rules and regulations.

That is the last thing I think now. As time went on I would cherish every opportunity I had to play at Lord's. I would watch as someone like Duncan Fletcher would take off his cap whenever he walked through the Long Room and I saw the respect in which the place was held by people from all over the world.

Now we are brilliantly looked after whenever we go to Lord's and nothing beats the feeling of arriving at headquarters on a Thursday morning, seeing the members queuing outside, or on a Saturday when you hear the champagne corks popping from an early stage. The only thing I would change is for the lift in the J.P. Morgan Media Centre to be a little quicker!

It is my pleasure, too, to write the foreword for this celebration of the Lord's collection. There are some fascinating, amazing stories in here which all cricket fans will relish. May Lord's always be that fantastic mix of the old and the new. It really is special.

*Nasser Hussain*

**Sir Spencer's Gargoyle, 1889**
**Photographed by Graham Morris, 2009**
When the famous terracotta façade of the Pavilion was first built, it was decorated with gargoyles said to be taken from MCC Committee members; only Lord Harris and Sir Spencer Ponsonby-Fane (see pp.28–9) have been identified.

*George Finch, 9th Earl of Winchilsea* by Nathaniel Dance, RA (1771) Purchased by MCC at Christie's in 1989

Winchilsea is pivotal in the story of Lord's: it was he who motivated and underwrote Thomas Lord's search for a new cricket ground. Fittingly his family is linked by marriage with that of A.J. Drexel, native of Philadelphia (the spiritual home of cricket in America), friend to Junius Morgan, and mentor to and business partner of his son J. Pierpont Morgan.

George. arl of Winchilsea s Nottingham.

# Sponsor's Foreword

In 2011, J.P. Morgan became a main sponsor at Lord's, the celebrated Home of Cricket.

Our sponsorship of the iconic Media Centre at Lord's gives J.P. Morgan an exceptional opportunity to support a classic international sport at a beloved UK institution. It also helps MCC carry on its cricket-related projects around the world. MCC has helped spur the rapid rise of cricket in Afghanistan, for example, and has supported rebuilding in Sri Lanka after the 2004 tsunami. For us, this is at the heart of a beneficial sponsorship: when two institutions can come together to do something terrific.

Lord's itself is an inspiration to cricket players, professionals and amateurs alike, and in 2011 we were fortunate enough to enjoy the first-ever private match played on the main ground. It was an event remarkable not only for its rarity but for the awe and wonder experienced by our clients who had come from all over the world to play – from India, South Africa, Australia, Singapore, Hong Kong, UAE, the US and Canada. Walking out on the pitch was, as one of them said, "something he had dreamed about his whole life."

It is a privilege for us to be a primary sponsor at Lord's and to be associated with MCC, the standard-bearer for the spirit of the game. This is an especially exciting time in cricket – the Australians come this year to England for an Ashes Series, the MCC Museum re-opens after refurbishment, and 2014 marks the celebration of the Bicentennial of the current Lord's Cricket Ground. We are delighted to be a part of it all.

We wish Lord's another 200 years of excellence in cricket.

*Jamie Dimon*
*Chairman and Chief Executive Officer*
*JPMorgan Chase & Co.*

J.P.Morgan

**Sachin Tendulkar by
David Buckland
Commissioned by MCC, 2002**
This was one of three photo
collages for MCC by the artist.
The format was intended to
defeat the practical difficulty
of international cricketers
finding time for suitably lengthy
sittings to portrait painters,
as well as to satisfy MCC's
desire to depict cricketers as
close to their playing careers
as possible. This composition
echoes beautifully those of
the early cricketing aristocrats,
in which backgrounds were
manipulated to provide a
suitable setting. Here the great
batsman is situated in the
middle of the Long Room on
one of its famous chairs with
the Committee Room beyond.

**William Wheateley, aged 14 by
Francis Alleyne (1786)
Donated to MCC by Sir
Jeremiah Colman, 1952**
The sitter in this picture was
not much younger than Sachin
Tendulkar when the latter
played his first Test Match. He
carries accurately depicted
stumps and bat, at a date not
long after the introduction of
the third stump. Francis Alleyne
was an itinerant portrait painter
who regularly visited country
houses, in whose collections
many of his works may still
be found. He specialised in
just such small oval three-
quarter length pictures, but
seems to have exhibited only
once, in 1790. The Wheateleys
lived at Lesney House in
Kent and Alleyne painted the
whole family.

11

**The Cricketers by Benjamin West, RA (1763)**
**On Loan from a Private Collection to MCC, courtesy of Robert Holden Ltd, 2012**
Born in Pennsylvania, Benjamin West was trained in Philadelphia, where he was sponsored by William Allen, reputedly the richest man in the city, before travelling to Italy. He arrived in London in 1763, the year in which it is thought this painting was commissioned. Allen was also in London at the time and his two sons are pictured here along with three fellow students. Remarkably the painting has remained in the Allen family until the present day. The composition is thought to derive from similar scenes painted by Nathaniel Dance of visitors to Italy, which West would have seen. Like Dance, he also produced copies for the various sitters, and a second painting (1764) commissioned by Ralph Izard still hangs in the Brook Club in New York. West was to spend the rest of his life in London, despite his close ties to those such as Benjamin Franklin. The sitters did return to America, fighting on different sides in the War of Independence, with Arthur Middleton one of the signatories of the Declaration of Independence. West went on to paint for the Royal Family before succeeding Sir Joshua Reynolds as the second President of the Royal Academy.

# Introduction

In 1987 Tony Lewis, celebrating MCC's Bicentenary, acknowledged the difficulty many face in differentiating the Club from its more famous home. When I arrived at Lord's, I too did not fully grasp the implications of the words "At Lord's today…", that the Ground was home to ICC and ECB, Middlesex and Marylebone. So writing in celebration of Lord's Bicentenary my aim has been to try to distinguish the one from the other, and in so doing to lay emphasis on the fabric of the place, the physical elements of what adds up to make Lord's what it is.

"I've been going there so long," wrote Tim Heald, not so many years ago, "that I feel it is always the same, even when – in detail – it manifestly isn't." I should like to draw attention to those details, grafted into the landscape of the Ground, or gathered by MCC and its Members, and use them to illuminate the wonderfully various and constantly changing nature of what is thought to be the most traditional of grounds, home to that most traditional of games. I intend to do this by drawing comparisons rather than by penning a chronological account, and hope that these similarities and contrasts prompt the first-time visitor and the familiar friend alike to draw some unexpected conclusions.

Navigating around Kew Gardens to visit an exhibition of the work of David Nash, I was struck by how wonderfully his bronze and charred wood sculptures brought out the very best in their vital and often vigorous surroundings. On reflection, such is the relationship of MCC's collections to their home. The modesty of the Ashes Urn sits in stark contrast to the pomp of an Ashes Test, and the J.P. Morgan Media Centre acts as an unlikely backdrop to a game

**Preparing the English Heritage plaque for the second Lord's Ground Instigated by Murad Qureshi, photographed by Clare Skinner, 2006**

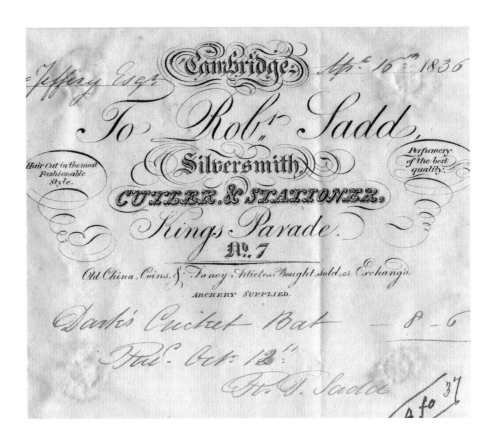

**Receipt for a James Dark bat Inscribed to Mr Jeffery from Robert Sadd, 1836**

of such antiquity; each gives its audience context and connects them to times past and future.

I received my own first taste of this when I attended the final round of interviews to succeed the retiring curator Stephen Green. I was ushered to a box in the Tavern Stand overlooking Middlesex in one of their early matches of the 2003 season. What seemed to be the whole of a committee was ranged along two tables facing the cricket. "We are looking for a new broom … someone to bring energy and a new dynamism … to create a museum for the future …" Moments later tradition reclaimed them as Ben Hutton, grandson of the great Sir Len, scored his maiden first-class century; my interviewers stepped out to applaud from the balcony. By way of farewell, Roger Knight shook my hand and, with what I hoped was a wry grin, said, "Good to meet you, pity you chose the wrong tie today."

In the Ground's earliest days, players arrived at Lord's kitted out in japanned "slippers", silk stockings and tight fitting-jackets trimmed with braid or ribbon, running the risk of rampant pickpockets. On field, they shunned pads and protective clothing as "unmanly", although it was the most dangerous pitch in the country, and suffered the instructions of their nobleman captains and, no doubt, retired grandees on the boundary edge. Betting tables at the pavilion steps stood witness to the purpose of the afternoon's play.

Two hundred years later, players rarely enter through the public gates but are shuttled individually by minders through Gate 6 from Grove End Road, past guards and dogs, to a "sealed" Dressing Room. They are uniformed both on and off the field, and their health and diet are constantly checked, in preparation for three hours, six hours, one day, four days or five days of cricket. It would be no surprise for an international player to wake up wondering where he or she is playing given the schedules and the distances travelled.

Yet once at Lord's, they can sense the history and traditions of this celebrated stage. It's not through detailed study, for such students of the game are few and far between – Adam Gilchrist was to be found jammed in among museum-goers on a wet morning of an Ashes Test, and Kumar Sangakkara rarely fails to give his teammates the "tour" whenever he plays here. It is just that Lord's exudes history: press conferences in the Museum, statues on the training ground, honours boards in the dressing room, jazz on the breeze …

**Original bookplate for the MCC Library Commissioned by MCC, designed by Forman, date unknown**

Each object I have picked for this book – some dusted down, some freshly unearthed – contributes to this resonance, builds this all-important context. Many are photographed for the first time in situ, on the Victorian leather-topped Pavilion tables, the Committee Room chairs, against the backdrop of a memorial plaque, a monogrammed bannister, a balcony railing. Each is a small brush-stroke in the overall impression that Lord's delivers.

One of the most challenging but enjoyable tasks I have faced as Curator has been to bring my personal experience to the tradition of commissioning player portraits. (Some of the most recent works are published for the first time in this book.) Each is at once an enduring image and yet a moment in time. A painter cannot successfully turn back the clock, he cannot paint authentically to another's taste; nor can he fudge the relationship he builds or fails to build with the sitter. In creating this book, I have likewise felt that it is very much a product of its time; it cannot hope to be comprehensive, it remains a portrait only.

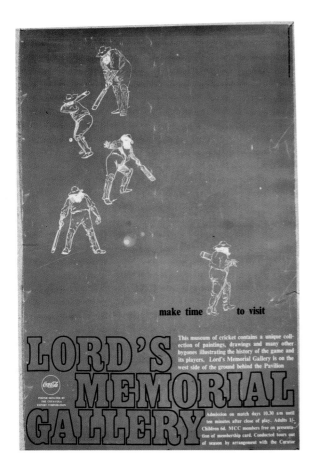

make time to visit

LORD'S MEMORIAL GALLERY

This museum of cricket contains a unique collection of paintings, drawings and many other bygones illustrating the history of the game and its players. Lord's Memorial Gallery is on the west side of the ground behind the Pavilion

Coca-Cola

POSTER DONATED BY THE COCA-COLA EXPORT CORPORATION

Admission on match days 10.30 a m until ten minutes after close of play. Adults 1/-, Children 6d. MCC members free on presentation of membership card. Conducted tours out of season by arrangement with the Curator

**Advertising poster for the Imperial Memorial Cricket Gallery Sponsored by Coca-Cola, 1967**

In 1914, the year before his death, the longest-serving member of MCC, Sir Spencer Ponsonby-Fane (see pp.28–9), recalled:

> Oh what changes I have seen and taken part in, not only in the scene itself but the nature and exponents of the game. It is only natural that in such a length of time such changes should have taken place, but it is almost impossible to compare the rough and simple habits of those times with the luxury of the present day.

Could he have anticipated the changes that have just taken place at Lord's in the space of one decade? The unrivalled euphoria of the 2005 Ashes Series, the ICC departing Lord's after 96 years, a World Twenty20 championship final, Pakistan "hosting" a Test Match, Allen Stanford flying in to rent the England team, Olympic archery, a Sunday morning betting scandal, and on top of this Father Time almost painted white.

No wonder then that each author of the various books on MCC and Lord's has shrunk from claims to a definitive history. The most recent was Stephen Fay's welcome description of the workings of Tom Graveney's Presidency (2006), in the vein of Niall Edworthy's somewhat controversial *Lord's: The Home of Cricket* (1993). Stephen Green's retirement after 35 years was marked by his gentle essay on *The Cathedral of Cricket* (2003) that looked to Tony Lewis's more extensive *Double Century* and Benny Green's omnivorous *Lord's Companion*, both published on the Club's Bicentenary (1987). Best of all perhaps is Geoffrey Moorhouse's "fair and meticulous" account of 1983 or, for a detailed annual description of the post-war period, Diana Rait Kerr and Ian Peebles' rigorous account.

If the pace of change limited the ambitions of these authors, they may also have felt the weight of landmark works by Sir Pelham Warner and Lord Harris, *eminences grises* of MCC, who were responsible for setting the tone of Lord's early hagiography. Lord Harris, for example, is thought to be responsible for the Ground's current all-pervading, but historically inaccurate epithet: "Home of Cricket". A reliance on previous histories of the Ground was surely enhanced by the disorganised state of the archive collection. While researchers such as Peter

Oborne, Bruce Murray and Ramachandra Guha mused that MCC may have been defensively unhelpful, it is rather the case that the Club was literally unprepared to satisfy exhaustive enquiry.

As a result, in spite of a period of unprecedented interest in sport's history, a consequence of the excitement of the Olympics, investigations have still failed to resolve once and for all the Club's foundation date, to uncover the momentous decision that brought about the change in the Club's colours from sky blue to scarlet and gold (the exact colours have only finally been described with the Club's incorporation by Royal Charter in 2013), or to trace either the history of the Club's most famous painting or of course the origin of the Ashes Urn.

The delightful *Treasures at Lord's* by Tim Rice (1989) and *Pavilions of Splendour*, primarily researched and written by James Offen (2004), are the only books to draw attention to the collections and architecture as an important part of the heritage of both game and Ground. I hope that *A Portrait of Lord's* takes their lead and goes further, focusing on the objects and artworks not simply as illustrations to a history, and not just as images of events and people. By exploring their own particular history, I hope it will solve some unanswered questions and approach the Ground's history from a fresh perspective.

Often in the museum world scant regard is paid to the private collector whose deep pockets so often outbid public institutions for works at auction and subsequently remove them from the public eye. For the history of sport, however, the private collector has been invaluable, for without him much that is still considered by museums as merely memorabilia would have been lost. MCC was itself just such a collector. Its willingness to acquire works and its nature as a Club seemed only to encourage donations, providing for a "common" good, albeit that of a limited membership. These gifts and purchases adorned the clubhouse until they outgrew it and a happy solution was found in combination with the establishment of a memorial dedicated to all cricketing victims of the Second World War.

An appeal for funding and fixtures for the "Memorial Gallery" drew donations from all levels of cricket, whether individuals, schools or clubs, and the first name in the donations book was that of the Duke of Edinburgh, who was present at the consecration ceremony led by the Bishop of London.

The spirit of the building is particularly resonant as it had been a racquets court before wartime damage, and would have been even more so had the original plan (of those practical times) for the reconstruction been effected: MCC had sought donations of various timbers from the international cricket boards, rather in the manner of the State Coach Britannia (which incidentally contains a small piece of wood from the beams of the original Lord's Hotel).

Since its inception the identity of the Gallery has slowly changed, largely in response to the instigation of popular public tours, in an attempt to provide a rather more educative and less simply reflective display. For many years it traced a chronology of the game, though perhaps too little was known of the early game to draw firm conclusions. The ongoing lack of disciplined collecting provided an irregular assortment of objects and for many years too little was made of the contemporary game.

However, exhibitions on Lord's itself, W.G. Grace, paintings and cartoons paved the way for further successful temporary displays on a variety of cricketing themes. Photographs by Patrick Eagar, the career of Brian Lara and the connections between baseball and cricket have drawn an ever-growing public to the MCC Museum, as it is now known. It is with thanks to our current sponsor, J.P. Morgan, that MCC is now able, for the first time in its 150-year collecting history, to provide an unprecedented array of objects, books and documents maintained in museum-quality conditions and yet accessible to the public. This book marks the opening of a two-year Bicentenary exhibition highlighting not only the "Crown Jewels" of the collection, but also some of the wonderful range of research projects that have benefited from the re-cataloguing and digitisation of the last three years. The recent refurbishment will also allow the Museum to act as a far more effective hub for enriching the the whole Ground with more innovative displays so that visitors may take away a stronger sense of Lord's identity, no matter how short their time here.

It would be remiss of me not to mention the one person who particularly realised the potential of the collection to the public and who strove to bring a discipline and ordered approach that 70 years later seems remarkable in its perspicacity. Diana Rait Kerr, who died aged 94 just before Christmas 2012, devised the classification scheme for the library which is still in use today, and her clear and detailed notes, ledgers and registers have formed an invaluable chronology without which, it is no exaggeration to say, the heritage of Lord's would be inexplicable. Her professional contribution, along with that of her "amateur" predecessor, Captain T.H. Carlton Levick, combined with the gifts, involvement and interest of so many MCC Members and cricket lovers, is responsible for the survival of the rich history of Lord's. I hope that their names and to some extent their characters shape this book and provide encouragement to visit the Ground and explore the collections at its heart.

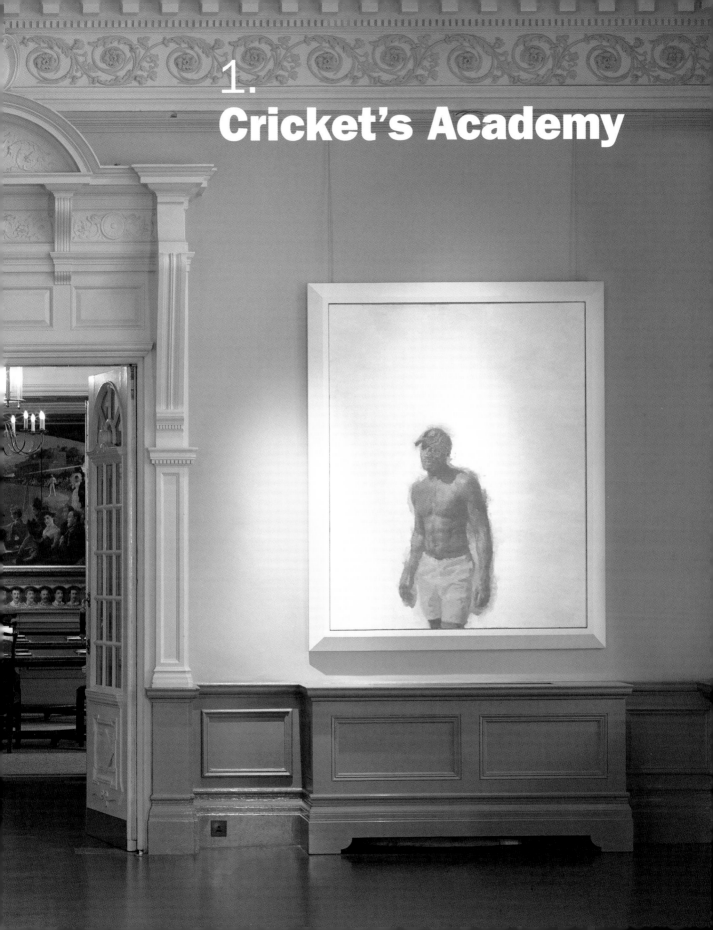

# 1.
# Cricket's Academy

"About half past one yesterday morning fire broke out in a large building called the Pavilion, erected in the cricket-ground near the school of the orphans of the clergy, on the St John's Wood Road. From the nature of the materials, which were chiefly of wood, although lately enlarged and beautified at great expense, the fire in a very short time defied the power of the fire-engines and water … So strong was the fire that the wooden rails round the building were partly destroyed. There was a very valuable wine cellar well stocked in the Pavilion … which shared the same fate with the building."
– *The Times, 30th July 1825*

So perished the early history of MCC and the early fabric of Lord's: scores, minutes and even the names of the early Presidents, which have never been rediscovered. It is clear, though, that the major loss was the wine cellar; it must have been felt hard by the Honorary Secretary who was himself a wine merchant, but was perhaps viewed with some relief by the previous thrifty tenant Thomas Lord, who supplied wine to the Club members through his wine shop at the entrance to the Ground.

Whatever art there may have been was of relatively little consequence, and over the next half century there is little mention of any acquisitions or holdings in the general inventories of the Club and Ground. Indeed cricket itself struggled through this period, with some twenty-odd matches per year providing insufficient profit either to support the membership or to provide upkeep of facilities. It was the introduction of a tennis court, shower rooms and billiard tables that prompted much needed membership numbers and consequent capital. Artwork did accumulate, but, according to the listing of 1907, the Tavern Hotel was full of hunting, shooting, racing and military prints, and the Long Room crowned with heads of waterbuck and antelope. Somewhere there even lurked a boa constrictor.

The first catalogue of the collection was pieced together in the early 1900s, written by the Treasurer Sir Spencer Ponsonby-Fane. It described the genesis of the collection as "no more than two" pictures that devolved to the Club when James Dark offered back the leasehold in 1864. Though hardly a collection, these two images were redolent of the early game. One of them is a painting after an original canvas that was designed as a decoration for a series of supper boxes in the notorious Vauxhall Pleasure Gardens. Such gardens,

Previous pages: Hanging in the Long Room are *Sir Viv Richards* by Brendan Kelly (2009) and *Brian Lara* by Justin Mortimer (2008). Beyond, in the Writing Room, is *An Imaginary Cricket Match at Lord's* by Robert Ponsonby Staples and George Barrable (1887; see p.28).

**Edward "Lumpy" Stevens by Mr Almond, itinerant artist (c.1783)**
**Private Collection**
This was commissioned by the Earl of Tankerville as one of series of portraits of the staff at his seat Knole in Kent. "Lumpy" was a celebrated bowler whose accuracy is credited for the introduction of the third stump.

hosting a variety of entertainments and centred on marquees or dining areas, had close associations with cricket. In the 1780s many of MCC's early members had played as the White Conduit Club, on three grounds next to a set of Gardens with a "Long Room" at its heart. The first Lord's Ground, founded in 1787, was situated on the new Marylebone Road, a stone's throw from the Yorkshire Stingo public house and gardens – named after a strong beer served there.

Vauxhall was the height of fashion, spiced with a disreputable renown, and the decorations were devised by two noted British artists, William Hogarth – supposed at one time to be the model for the wicketkeeper in this painting – and Francis Hayman, who started his career as scene designer at Drury Lane Theatre. The latter is specifically credited with the cricketing scene and, while the picture in the collections is only a crude copy, and the illustration shown here (see p.40) is only a print after Hayman's original, we get a fuller sense of his talents from the other beautiful picture which came to MCC.

Hayman had a studio in St Martin's Lane, where the first British Academy of painting was established by Hogarth, and he was instrumental along with Sir Joshua Reynolds in the subsequent formation of the Society of Artists of Great Britain, quickly incorporated by Royal Charter, and then the Royal Academy. It was in the work of this inaugural school of British painters and particularly those of St Martin's Lane that the first images of cricket appear.

Cricket was a fashionable hobby of the nobility, promoted by members of the Royal Family, and commonly held to be a "manly" game. It is not to be wondered that artists – from Reynolds's teacher Thomas Hudson to other Academy founders, such as Francis Cotes and Benjamin West – were quick to include references to the game. Whether suitable props appeared at the artists' own initiative or by popular demand, it can be argued that this correlation resulted in an early association of cricket and Britishness. Thus the 1752 print of Hayman's picture is accompanied by a verse extolling the British character. Francis Cotes's portrait of Lewis Cage (see p.30) pictures him fresh from a game with shirt unbuttoned and stocking down. Benjamin West paints his patron's sons, over from Philadelphia, with cricket bats as a souvenir of their stay in England (see pp.12–13). Most of these portraits picture children with the poise of gentlemen, imitating adulthood. Another American, John Singleton Copley, paints Richard Heber in this fashion during his stay in England.

The Swiss artist Jacques Sablet, however, depicts Thomas Hope in his twenties during his Grand Tour in Italy (p.222). The choice of Hope, who was to be one of the great tastemakers of his time, to have himself painted "at the wicket" was therefore a far more conscious decision.

This string of fashionable, expensive portraits was mirrored in the mass market where cricket entered the pictorial language of prints, lending itself to satire and caricature at all levels, from *Miss Wicket and Miss Trigger* (see p.219) to lampoons of society figures such as the Duke of Wellington. John Boydell, one of the most prominent print-sellers, had his best shop "at the sign of the cricket bat", just off St Martin's Lane.

Even outside the capital cricket's popularity was evident, as reflected in pictures both anonymous and specific by itinerant artists: "Lumpy" Stevens, arguably the finest bowler of the time, was included in a series of servants' portraits at Knole in Kent by a Mr Almond, and a certain Henry Daw chose to be depicted in cricketing costume by Antonio Varres in Christchurch in Dorset (p.220).

This range of depiction stretches all the way to late Victorian England both in terms of its iconography and its association with Academicians. W.G. Grace "sat" in just such a gentleman's pose at Lord's for Archibald Stuart Wortley, and Philip Calderon's image of a child batting was translated into a sentimental mass market advertising image by the Pears Company (p.31). The walls of Lord's bear additional portraits by Nathaniel Dance, Sir William Beechey, Frank Holl and Willi Soukop, as well as pictures with a more directly cricketing subject by Sir Robert Ponsonby Staples, Albert Chevallier Tayler and William Bowyer.

It must be admitted that the game itself, though wonderfully aesthetic in many ways, does present a significant challenge to an artist. Diana Rait Kerr in her essay on MCC and the Arts went so far as to say that it remained "an unrewarding subject for an artist, and the number of modern painters who have portrayed it successfully is very small indeed". Viscount Ullswater, in his tour of the Long Room as part of Pelham Warner's book on Lord's, concentrated to no small extent on the challenging perspectives, the unrealistic shades of grass and the absence

*A Cricket Sight Board* by **L.S. Lowry (1964–9) Private Collection, loaned to Lord's in 2005** This is part of a picture which the artist himself cut into two pieces, unhappy with the overall composition. He worked for five years without resolving the differences between this more typical work and that of the match itself.

**A match between the
Royal Artillery and the
Hundonsbury Club,
photographed by
Roger Fenton (1857)
The Priory Collection**
This is acknowledged to be the
earliest photograph of cricket;
it was taken by the Ian Botham
of early photography, a true
allrounder, who took pictures
of landscapes, architecture,
the Crimean war, the British
Museum collections and
royal portraits. He lived a
stone's throw from Lord's in
Primrose Hill.

of fielders in positions they really ought to have occupied. Yet William Worsley, as President, donated a picture of cricket near the smoking chimneys of Stoke-on-Trent by Adrian Allinson in order to encourage the acquisition of modern works for the Ground.

Although Sir Spencer was less than discriminating in his searches for cricket images, in his own words "ransacking every dealer's shop in London and elsewhere", MCC has been very fortunate in the quality of donations and purchases that have allowed it, the previous criticisms nothwithstanding, to display a variety of winning representations. Many of the most successful take place on or around the field but not in the midst of play. An intriguing eighteenth-century drawing delights with its comic moments (p.42), Robert James's famous chimney sweeps toss a bat to decide who fields first, the Excelsior Cricket Club chair their hero from the field (p.32) and Albert Chevallier Tayler in *Eton v Harrow* singles out a lone fielder at the boundary's edge hemmed in by a ring of spectators.

The earliest successful efforts to depict a game in play owe a debt to perhaps the most familiar of all on-field images, Hayman's *Cricket in Marylebone Fields* of c.1740. Alternatively labelled as the "Royal Academy Club", its importance lies not in who plays or where it is situated but its accurate portrayal of the contemporary game. Its iconography was used for the handkerchiefs on which the early Laws are delineated (p.203), for the frontispiece to the first copies of the printed Laws, and for many other painted and engraved scenes such as that on the so-called "Thomas Lord Bowl" (p.38).

Henry Walton's picture of the Mason brothers in 1771 (see detail, p.33) is a noteworthy successor as a truthful portrait of the game. The batsman faces you, the viewer, as if you were the bowler, while his brother crouches low behind the stumps. The pitch is worn, the bat, stumps and costumes exactly of the period, and in the distance one of the "fielders" apes the bowler's pose. The landscape, I am told, is recognisably that of Harrow, and the boy's patron Ambrose Humphreys stands as "umpire". It is a rare picture and altogether convincing as the forerunner of a cricket genre.

L.S. Lowry's *Cricket Match*, which was displayed at Lord's in 2005, is an example of the challenges of synthesising a successful cricket scene. The artist battled to resolve this composition for five years before finally cutting it into two separate parts; by his own admission he felt that the foreground image of the crowd (p.24) worked far better without the pitch and players behind.

The challenge was just as great for the early photographers such as Roger Fenton, whose images of cricket are the earliest recognised. Admittedly his approach to the camera was far more like that of an artist to his canvas, and the perspectives of distant on-field play just as difficult to capture. Some of the more striking later images are those in the famous series by George Beldam that include Victor Trumper and Ranjitsinhji; Beldam freezes "action" to produce wonderfully melodramatic and wholly unrealistic moments.

The character of modern photography, film and television, shaped by the dramatic technological innovations of the last 30 years, has resulted in an altogether different approach. Their unerring accuracy has once again given more scope to the painted image. That is not to say that the challenge of interpreting play has diminished, rather that the artist has more freedom to experiment, focusing on individual aspects of the game rather than trying to present the entire scene.

For each different type of media Lord's has proved a wonderful academy and in this respect has found its place in the artistic traditions of St John's Wood. It is noticeable that the rhythm of the area's artistic heyday matched the pinnacle of cricket's popularity. When W.G. Grace began to frequent Lord's, neighbouring roads boasted the finest artists, such as Lawrence Alma-Tadema, James Tissot, Edwin Landseer and the group known as the St John's Wood Clique. Roger Fenton lived a short distance away in Primrose Hill.

MCC continues to collect and sponsor artists, drawing upon the natural grandeur of its situation as well as the appeal and challenge of the game. The wonderfully catholic nature of the membership, including such figures as the late Sir Oliver Millar, Surveyor of the Queen's Pictures, has attracted Academician after Academician, so much so that, from artists to sculptors to architects, the connection has been translated into the very fabric of Lord's.

*Holyday* **by James Tissot
(c.1876)**
**Tate Gallery Collection**
This painting is set in the artist's garden in St John's Wood, recognisable by its distinctive cast-iron colonnade enclosing a large ornamental fishpond. This picture of young people flirting was considered by some to be rather vulgar. The I Zingari club cap is a prominent feature.

# Collecting Cricket

Were one to try to caricature an MCC Member of days gone by, one would struggle to imagine a character more perfect than Sir Spencer Cecil Brabazon Ponsonby-Fane, GCB ISO, Gentleman Usher to the Sword of State and Comptroller of the Lord Chamberlain's Office. Owner of Brympton D'Evercy, "the most incomparable house in Britain" and setting for his annual cricket parties, he was nominated for membership by the Secretary Benjamin Aislabie and was related in marriage to the President Frederick Beauclerk.

*An Imaginary Cricket Match at Lord's* **by Robert Ponsonby Staples and George Barrable (1887, detail)**
**Purchased from the artist by MCC, 1927**
This detail of the largest painting in the MCC collection portrays Sir Spencer Ponsonby-Fane, its "founder", in pensive mood in his light grey top hat.

Sir Spencer first played for MCC as a boy of fifteen, soon after round-arm bowling was legalised, and "... Mr Dark, then proprietor of the Ground ... presented me with a bat and the 'Freedom of the Ground', as he called it". He died in the same year as W.G. Grace, aged 91, still Treasurer and Trustee, having served on the Committee for three lengthy terms and on the Tennis Committee that drew up the first rules of lawn tennis.

In honour of his service to the Club, his portrait was commissioned and painted by William Ouless, RA, but he is probably better recognised, in a distinctive beige suit, together with his fellow founders of I Zingari, in the painting by Lowes Cato Dickinson. Perhaps more fittingly still, for a man who laid the foundation stone of the Pavilion, his likeness is disguised as one of the gargoyles on the terracotta façade (see p.6). Writing in the text of the revised catalogue of the paintings of 1912, he claims responsibility for forming the nucleus of the collection from 1864 when MCC acquired several pictures as part of the leasehold of the Ground. Despite a seeming paucity of material, during his unstinting term as Treasurer – turning down the Presidency on more than one occasion – he appears to have been free to propose and support the Club's investment in the collections for the next half century. By the time he died in post the Club had over 500 works of art and objects in its collection.

**Sir Spencer, "The Guv'nor"**
**From the I Zingari scrapbooks,**
**1903**
The founders of I Zingari, who included Sir Spencer, appointed a perpetual "President" who remained in post even after he died. As a consequence the leader of the Club was known as the Governor.

**_Lewis Cage_ by Francis Cotes, RA (1768)**
**Purchased privately by MCC, 2010**

This "swagger" portrait of a young nobleman, mentioned in the letters of Jane Austen, hails from cricket's heartland in Kent and is a quintessential image at Lord's. Painted by one of the most fashionable portraitists of the day and founder of the Royal Academy in his studio in Marylebone, the original was finally acquired from the collection of John Paul Getty by MCC in 2010. Two copies had previously hung at Lord's: the first produced in 1908 by Eleanor Hughes D'Aeth, whose family then owned the painting; the second was commissioned by MCC in 1950 with permission from the then owner Lord Brocket.

**_Captain of the XI_ by Philip Hermogenes Calderon, RA (1882)**
**Loaned from the Priory Collection, 2012**

This picture was bought by the Managing Director of A.F. Pears and used to great effect as a marketing image, both on its products and in its _Pears' Annual_, which was produced with prints that might be individually framed. It is one of the most recognisable of cricket pictures and is on public view at Lord's for the first time for over 80 years. Philip Hermogenes Calderon was not only an Academician but also the first British artist to receive the Légion d'honneur. He became Keeper of Collections at the Royal Academy, and was a leading light in a group of artists who styled themselves the St John's Wood Clique, well known for their humour and practical jokes.

**The Winner of the Match by Henry Garland (1864) Donated to MCC by Mrs H. Doubleday, 1959**
In this sentimental Victorian genre scene the artist avoids the pitfalls of painting a game in progress, with the beauty of the scene complicated by the space between players and a challenging perspective. He brings the victorious young players and predominantly female spectators into close proximity, leaving the wonderful view – typical of the countryside around his birthplace of Winchester – as a backdrop. In the foreground he places a still life of equipment, which crops up in a surprising number of early pictures, although instead of the usual scorers we have a small family group. The vibrant colour gives the lie to the customary scene of whites against a green sward.

**Cricketers at Harrow School by Henry Walton (c.1771, detail) Acquired by MCC from Dickinson Roundell, 2011**
This picture, a notable recent acquisition, marks a significant change in the early depiction of cricket. This genre scene is as much about the game as about the sitters: a batsman with professionally made bat of correct proportion, a worn pitch, a wicketkeeper with hat to stop the ball, fitting costumes and even the distant figures describing the act of bowling. The painting stands as exceptional testimony to the time-honoured tradition of cricket in one of the great English public schools and is all the more unusual among such depictions in that we know the names of the three principal sitters. At the time of its commission, Walton was studying under the influential Johan Zoffany, and the painting illustrates Zoffany's technique and composition. Walton went on to become a dealer and art expert of great repute.

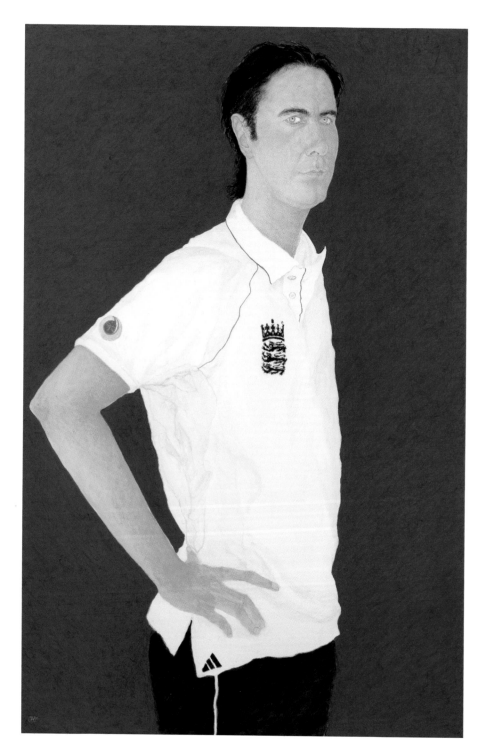

**Michael Vaughan
by Jennifer McRae
Commissioned by MCC, 2009**
As arguably England's most successful captain, Michael Vaughan was an obvious choice for MCC's commissioning scheme, which was established to capture the character of today's top cricketers, so often masked by media glare or the barriers of sunglasses and helmets during play. Meeting Vaughan for the first time at Headingley, the artist Jennifer McRae was struck by the colour of his eyes which came to play a formative role in the painting. His penetrating stare and angular pose reflect his competitive and prickly on-field personality, while the delicacy of the brushwork works well to describe his fine features and the light sheen of the shirt's modern fabric.

**Frank Woolley by Wilhelm Soukop, RA (c.1960)
Donated to MCC by
Mrs Woolley, 1988**
This bronze is pictured in front of the museum's war memorial plaque. The artist's own father took his life after his experiences in the First World War, and he himself was interned during the 1940s. In an industrious career he never settled to one style, reflecting, "I haven't stopped playing". One might apply this equally to Frank Woolley, such was his career: second only to Jack Hobbs for total career runs and to W.G. for matches in which he scored a century and took ten wickets. Debuting in the pre-1914 Golden Age, he retired months before the Second World War and was memorably summarised: "There was all summer in a stroke by Woolley."

***Presentation of Colours to
the 3rd Regiment, Royal East
India Volunteers at Lord's,
1797, engraved by W. Griggs
after the painting by Henry
Matthews, acquired by MCC
before 1907***
***Cannonball from the
Battle of Alma, Sebastopol,
1854, donated to MCC
by W. Higgins, 1923***
The Ground's early history
bears testament not only
to the entrepreneurial drive
of its tenant Thomas Lord,
but also to prevailing social

circumstances. Ballooning
and archery often gave way
to parades of the regiments
of volunteers as the country
twitched nervously against the
Napoleonic military threat. Just
over 50 years later, the Guards
were cricketing against the Leg
of Mutton ("the Rest") in the
Crimea as Britain joined France
to take on Russia. The pair
of cannonballs were donated
perhaps in memory of the
part Lord's hospital played in
treating the wounded veterans
from the Crimea.

*A Cricket Match between the Greenwich and Chelsea Hospital Pensioners* by Henry Alken (c.1825), donated to MCC by Jeremiah Colman, 1952
Porcelain mug, bequeathed to MCC by E. Rockley Wilson, 1957
Alken, like Soukop, was of European descent (Danish) and born into a family of artist/craftsmen. He was the archetypal sporting artist and lived in a flat above publisher Thomas McLean's "Repository of Wit and Humour" in Haymarket. Although not as bitingly satirical as some of his contemporaries, he was renowned for his humour and here pictures the kind of game reported widely in the press. The earliest match between one-armed and one-legged cricketers was reported in 1796. The interest generated was such that the perimeter fence was swept away in the crush and the match delayed for over three hours.

**A Chinese export-porcelain punch bowl (c.1786)**
**Acquired by MCC from S. Marchant & Son, 1984**

Much that is known about Thomas Lord is conjecture. He is credited with Jacobite roots and a passionate love for the game of cricket, but there is no proof of the former and he was quite ready to sell off Lord's for development to fund his retirement. Ownership of this singular porcelain bowl is also attributed to him. Commissioned from Jingdezhen and probably decorated in Canton, it bears three cricketing scenes taken from the famed Hayman painting (see p.40). The attribution to Lord is conjured from the East Indiaman inside the bowl which bears the legend "Thirx" (Thirsk is his birthplace). Though purchased in 1984, serious research is only now being undertaken.

***England's Twelve Champion Cricketers*, 1859**
**Donated to MCC by J.C. Boyle or E. St G. Hewitson, 1939/41**

This print is one of the best known of early cricket images, with the players posing as a team on the deck of the *Nova Scotia* just before sailing to Quebec from Liverpool on 7th September 1859. Photographs of cricket are among the earliest taken in Britain, of which the best were taken by Roger Fenton. The 1859 Tour was received rapturously in the USA but the Civil War then delayed a return until 1868, by which time it was a baseball game between the tourists and an American side that brought the biggest crowd in a decade to the St George Ground, New York City.

**Cricket, engraved by
B. Cole after the painting
by Francis Hayman
Published by New Universal
Magazine, 1752**

Several paintings of the same scene depicted in this print exist but it is thought that the original has not survived. It is believed to have been painted by Francis Hayman as one of several pleasure scenes to decorate arbours in the infamously disreputable Vauxhall Pleasure Gardens. This origin is ironically at odds with the verses accompanying the earlier version of the print by C. Benoist, which end: "Britons, whom Nature has for War design'd / In the soft Charms of Ease no Joy can find / Averse to wast in Rest th'inviting Day / Toil forms their Game & Labour is their Play."

**Eighteenth-century cricket bat
Donated to MCC by the 6th
Duke of Buccleuch, 1912**

There is no doubt that private patronage was crucial to both the game itself and its pictorial depiction. Cricket was a fashionable means of gambling for the nobility, who encouraged the recruitment of specialist players to their staffs and customised equipment; in this case a bat belonging to 4th Duke of Buccleuch (1772–1812) is stamped with a coronet and the letter D for Dalkeith. Nobles' adoption of the game did not extend, at least in the middle of the eighteenth century, to the use of cricket bats in their own portraits, but bats did appear as props in the depiction of their young sons. Efforts have been made to trace the development of the bat through such pictures, but this avenue of research has proved unreliable in anything but the broadest sense.

**Cricketing scene drawn in chalk by an unknown artist (c.1740s)**
**Acquired by MCC, before 1907**
This fascinating drawing depicts not only children playing cricket but also the typical landscape and activities that surround a game. In the background, below a windmill, a bout of boxing takes centre stage with a crowd of interested and interesting onlookers; to the left a furtive exchange is taking place, while to the right edge a man relieves himself. This generic scene is familiar from engravings and illustrations as well as designs for ceramic objects. This individual drawing, however, remains a mystery, and reflects how ripe for research the collections still remain.

**Maquette for *The Bowler* by Antony Dufort**
**Commissioned by MCC, 2000**
With the funds raised from the successful Bicentenary auction in 1987, a decision was taken to commission two statues, representing the batsman and bowler, to be situated within the Ground. After much discussion, it was agreed that neither should depict a particular cricketer. The preliminary sketches for *The Bowler* explored many actions including those of Max Walker, Lance Gibbs, Jeff Thomson and Fred Trueman (see p.98), and there was also much debate at Committee about that of Alec Bedser, but it was that of Dennis Lillee that formed the template for the final dynamic sculpture.

**The Appeal** by Lawrence Toynbee (1976)
**Acquired by MCC from The Fine Art Society, 1995**

A true sports artist, Toynbee's work included boxing, rowing, rugby, football as well as cricket. Born in the 1920s, he went on to play for Oxford at Lord's in 1942, but it was perhaps the influence of another painter, Anthony Fry, that enabled him to capture the rhythm and spirit of a game so successfully. His work was exhibited by the Fine Art Society in 1984 and 1985, and MCC went on to acquire a substantial collection of paintings, though the notable *Nursery End at Lord's* was presented by the FAS to the York Museums Trust.

***Last Ball* by Andy Pankhurst
Commissioned by MCC, 2002**
Chairman of MCC Lord
Alexander of Weedon
introduced Andy Pankhurst
to Lord's to paint portraits of
Michael Atherton and Alec
Stewart on their attaining 100
Test caps. Pankhurst then
travelled as MCC's "Young
Artist", given the opportunity
to tour with the English Test
team. His particular talent,
encouraged by the example of
Euan Uglow, for planes of bright
yet subtle colour, suited the
harsh light of Australia and this,
his most memorable image,
captured Steve Waugh scoring
a boundary off the last ball of
the day to reach his century.

# Sitting for a Portrait

There is no hard and fast rule as to whose portrait hangs at Lord's: "Our policy is not to have a policy." Most England captains, but not all; why not Verity or Larwood? Posthumous pictures miss the point of portraiture; they lack the vim and vigour of a face to face encounter. What about Cook? His time will come. Only one England player in modern times – Alec Stewart – has walked out to play and passed his portrait on the way.

*Nasser Hussain* **by James Lloyd Commissioned by MCC, 2008**
Nasser sat for the artist not long after he made a hundred against New Zealand in his final Test at Lord's. His retirement proved just as frenetic as his cricketing career and the portrait was painted from a sole sitting.

Players' experiences of the portrait process vary greatly. "It was very weird for me to sit to have my portrait painted," said Nasser Hussain. "I'm usually the sort of person who runs around at 100mph chasing my tail. I found it a struggle to sit still for an hour and I kept getting told off by the artist for moving around." In fact Nasser managed only one full sitting and the artist included that sketch in the finished picture, making a point, perhaps.

In comparison, Graham Gooch's was a marathon performance: "I sat for four days for my portrait in my living room in my home in Essex at the end of the season. I quite like it, but a lot of people don't. It's quite quirky – my face is sort of screwed up on one side! I'm wearing the old blazer and sweater. My final two tours for England were the last when we wore the old blazer with the braiding on. The cream sweater featured just the crown, no three lions. You cannot compare them with the new white fleeces. The wool sweaters are much treasured."

Andy Pankhurst was "not really a portrait painter" when asked to depict Michael Atherton and Alec Stewart; he viewed it as an artistic challenge. Michael Henderson reviewed the pictures for the *Daily Telegraph*: "Atherton looks intense, Stewart slightly agitated, as though he can't wait to put his pads on and have a bat. At first the works seem unremarkable, but half close your eyes, take away 500 years, imagine Atherton in a cloak, with a chain of office round his neck, and there is something of Holbein's portrait of Sir Thomas More about that unrelenting gaze."

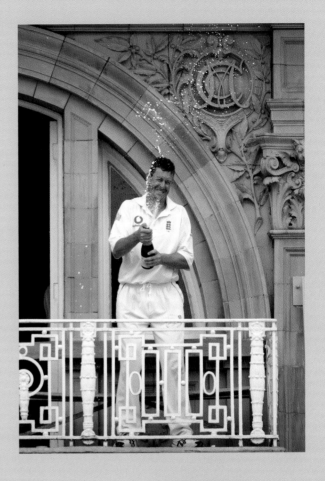

**Ashley Giles on the players' balcony**
**Photographed by**
**Philip Brown, 2004**
In July 2004 he recorded match-figures of 9–210 in the first Test at Lord's (including his 100th Test wicket, Brian Lara), which won him the Man of the Match award and a place on the Honours Board – but not a portrait.

# 2.
# A Sense of Place

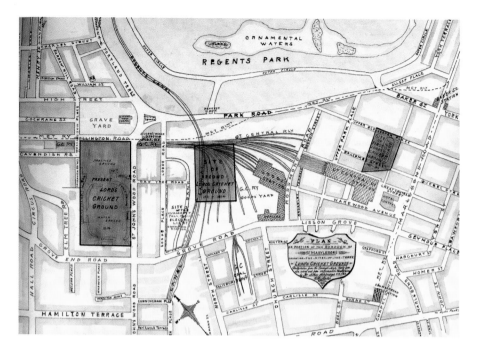

**Plan of St Marylebone (detail) by W.H. Slatter (1902)**
This hand-drawn plan by William Slatter, MCC Clerk of Works, is one of many of his drawings and plans at Lord's. This shows the locations of all three of Thomas Lord's Grounds after the move from Islington, as well as the old Lord's Tube station, which closed in 1939, and Pall Mall power station.

Although the reputation of Lord's conjures up impressions of grandeur, the approach to the Ground even on a match day promises relatively little. Queues wrap around the seemingly impermeable wall and it is only when one is at last squeezed through the defensive rank of turnstiles that the joy of Lord's is suddenly and refreshingly evident. It is hard to imagine that the Ground as we know it has been shaped so markedly by its environs.

Variously dubbed the cathedral and the Mecca of cricket, Lord's is fittingly situated within sight of a surprisingly varied series of temples. Land for the Central London Mosque was made available in Hanover Gate in the 1940s and the dome was eventually raised in 1977. It overlooks the site of Lord's unpopular second Ground, and the Regent's Canal which forced its move – not to the dissatisfaction of either Club or tenant (Thomas Lord was handsomely compensated). St John's Wood Church, facing the mosque on the northern bank of the canal, was designed and built in the same year as that move to the current site, and the celebrations were hosted by Lord, a vestryman, in the Pavilion of his new Ground over the Wellington Road.

Turning south-west down St John's Wood Road past Winchilsea House, Lord's View and Pavilion Apartments, one has no inkling of the enormous power station so obvious to spectators in the 1930s and so detrimental to the Club's art collection that all the pictures had to be glazed. These large apartment blocks

Previous pages: St John's Wood Churchyard, photographed by Graham Morris, 2011. In 1814 Thomas Lord offered the Pavilion at the newly acquired Lord's Ground for the consecration celebrations upon the completion of the church designed by Thomas Hardwick. The view of the trees in the churchyard, cherished by MCC Members, has come to shape the development of the Ground.

do however give an inkling of a previous era of development that occurred as Lord's found its feet. Taking advantage of leases expiring in Regent's Park, John Nash set out to design a royal masterplan which came to fruition as Thomas Lord retired. He looked to take advantage by selling to developers, and only swift and decisive action by William Ward secured an ample home for MCC. As James Dark took on the tenancy at Lord's in 1835, the Regent's Park opened to the public. Two years later, MCC celebrated its golden jubilee in muted fashion as the King's funeral was held.

At the south-west corner of Lord's stands the Liberal Jewish Synagogue. It was designed at almost exactly the same time as the Grace Gate opposite and although it was redeveloped after it suffered a direct hit in the war, the original portico still stands. As a consequence of the damage the Sabbath services were for a time held in the Pavilion. The current Rabbi confesses that his congregation know what to expect of him during a Lord's Test; his Sabbath sermons are short and pithy.

Around the corner in Lisson Grove, one finds the Church of Our Lady, one of the first Roman Catholic churches built after the Emancipation Act of 1829, which appears in all the early illustrations of the Ground. Labelled a Regency classic by John Betjeman, it was funded by the daughters of the manager of Royal Opera House, Sir John Gallini. Development means it now lies just out of sight.

This multi-faith community sits on an ancient landscape full of Anglo-Saxon heritage. Covered originally by the great forest of Middlesex, it was owned, as the name suggests, by the Knights of St John. This ancient heritage is still represented in the badge of Middlesex County Cricket Club. Lord's protects and cherishes the tradition of the team, marooned by the formal abolition of its county in

**Original study for the Warner Stand mural by Robin and Christopher Ironside (c.1958)**
Robin was self-taught, and deputy keeper at the Tate Gallery, while Christopher taught fine art and worked on the Festival of Britain, the Coronation and the 1964 Shakespeare commemoration. They combined for this design after completing stage sets for the Royal Opera House for both ballet (*Sylvia*) and opera (*Der Rosenkavalier*).

1965. The seaxes of the county insignia point to military traditions, and certainly when Thomas Lord moved into the area such connections were still strong. The New Artillery Barracks, completed in 1812 on the site of the Old Farm, were supplemented by a cavalry riding school six years later; hooves could then be heard from 1880 until 2012, as latterly the King's Troop Royal Horse Artillery paraded to exercise in Regent's Park. They would pass the park's eastern corner where Grove House still stands, designed by Decimus Burton, one of eight villas realised of the original 56 planned by Nash. The artist Sigismund Goetze converted the stables to a wonderful studio that rivalled those of pre-eminent Victorian artists James Tissot, Edwin Landseer and Lawrence Alma-Tadema on St John's Wood and Grove End roads.

The early nineteenth century was the beginning of the area's increasing sub-urbanisation, and swathes of elegant Regency terraces sprang up in response to the plans in and around Regent's Park. As a consequence of this development, Lord's and its neighbouring land was always under threat, but prolonged vigilance and determined attempts to bolster its boundaries secured the immediate vicinity by 1929.

*Oxford v Cambridge at Lord's* **by H.W. Marshall (1885)**
This beautiful watercolour is an accurate panorama of the Ground before the current Pavilion was built in 1890. From left to right can be seen the old real tennis court, Lord's Hotel, Luncheon Rooms, built in 1881, and the long low "Q" stand.

Of these nineteenth-century terraces, the closest survivors are in Baker Street, where one plays home to the Sherlock Holmes museum at 221b. The character was dreamed up by MCC member Sir Arthur Conan Doyle, who lived, at one time, a short walk to the south. He named his eponymous hero after cricketers employed at Lord's (see pp.196–7). Nearby Abbey Road is also still lined with houses built in the 1830s, one of which was converted to the famous studios in 1931, opening with Elgar and the London Symphony Orchestra, and from 1962 to 1970 hosting of course The Beatles, who recorded almost continuously on that spot.

Despite this constant development, and perhaps because of its name, St John's Wood has always been considered rather out-of-town, a verdant land of stately villas with a somewhat bucolic feel. This was surely helped by its reputation for market gardens. Nearby Maida Vale had some of the largest in London including one that survives to this day: Clifton Nurseries, founded in 1851, and run by Mr Krupp, an apprentice artist gardener to the Kaiser, had the biggest Palm House of the 1880s bar that of Kew Gardens.

According to William Slatter's memoirs, Henderson's, or the "Pine Apple Nursery" as it was also known, abutted Lord's and was renowned for both its

fruit and flowers. When tulips were the rage in the 1850s and 1860s, it was said that visitors' carriages thronged the Wellington Road to see his shows. MCC purchased the nursery and added it to Lord's, providing a feature that remains exceptional. As access to the main Ground has been curtailed, this Nursery Ground has served both spectators and players of more modest skills with a place to stretch their legs.

At the opposite, western boundary of the Ground, the Harris Garden provides a taste both of the Kentish weald and the courtyard garden. It was planned as a cloister by Sir Herbert Baker, but his ideas found no favour with the MCC Committee and only the fine flint wall was built, with stone from Lord Harris's estate. It is a fitting if understated connection to the ancient wood (weald) that covered the valley between the Downs in what was cricket's original heartland.

To the north the Coronation Gardens, renovated in 1952, provide a shady tree-lined area, reminiscent perhaps of the extensive gardens of Sir Edwin Landseer, which once were here. This corner is home

to the hamper. Looking down from the Library windows, the match-day patchwork of rugs stretches under the London planes and chestnuts, the copper beech and weeping ash (dedicated to Billy Griffith).

Close at hand is the coach mound, around which carriages used to make their turn. This too is planted with specimens: eucalyptus (dedicated to Keith Miller) and quince (a gift from the Worshipful Company of Grocers). From here the privileged, perched high up on their carriage seats, might have glimpsed the cricket over the old Q stand, beloved of Neville Cardus (see p.198). Here too in the 1850s the elder Ground boys used to wait on ropes tethered between the trees, attending the visitors' horses; the juniors could not be trusted to restrain them when startled by the noises of the game.

To the north-east was the pen that held up to 400 sheep, kept for a weekend's cropping before delivery to Smithfield Market on a Monday. With freedom to wander when a match was not in play, they did much damage to the pitch in wet conditions. On one occasion, thought to be burglars, they were chased out of the

**Mound Stand**
**Inauguration Plaque**
**Unveiled by Duke of Edinburgh,**
**Bicentenary Test Match, 1987**
Built to celebrate the Club's Bicentenary, Michael Hopkins's design used the fine brick arcade of the old stand designed by Frank Verity in 1898 and additional reclaimed bricks (London Stocks) dating from 1857.

professionals' rooms at gun point by James Dark. Deer kept them company for a time, though they reportedly came to unfortunate ends: perhaps unsurprisingly, one was hit and fatally injured by a cricket ball.

Geese too were kept for cropping and used as late as 1915. They must have relished the ponds of the early years in front of the Mound Stand and Grandstand sites in which Steven Slatter (James Dark's right-hand man) learnt to swim with a rope around his waist. They were fed by natural springs that also supported wells under the pavilion. Apparently their outline could still be seen in very dry summers even after they were filled in.

In his book *Double Century* Tony Lewis describes the Ground being run by the Dark family as folk might run a fairground. They certainly had to drum up custom as there were as few as nine matches in a season. Facilities were correspondingly spare and it was only with the investment of the forbidding tennis court that visitor numbers rose.

Building only really began after the Club secured the freehold (1866) and even then, after the cost of constructing the new Tavern in 1867, it sought a consortium of investors to take on the addition of a new Grandstand until profits were assured. Luncheon rooms were added in 1881. As the crowds kept coming so extra refreshment rooms were added, and from 1902 the famous arbours were plumbed in along the perimeter wall. This was the high point of the Edwardian scene, the golden pre-war age: carriages and arbours, toppers and crinolines, dining and perambulation.

War intervened twice, but the crowds returned to celebrate the peace and revel in a familiar scene. The landscape grudgingly adapted to the modern era as cricket lost its sparkle and short-term gains and a lack of vision hampered a new plan. It was only as the Club approached its Bicentenary, sensibly coerced into significant investment by enlightened Members, that a new spectating experience dawned. The imminent celebration must have fostered the plans, and Michael Hopkins's new Mound Stand was realised thanks to a carefully solicited donation from John Paul Getty. Not only did he agree to meet half of the original costs, but when the project overran he wrote out a cheque within a week for his further "half". His seal of approval was to take a box, at full price, for the rest of his cricket-watching days.

The Mound Stand was followed by multiple new stands, the Cricket Academy and the Media Centre. This left the Members a little bereft as the Pavilion had not been renovated since its creation in 1889. This was rectified in 2004–5 when it was restored to its former glory with facilities to suit a membership of over 15,000 and a profile that matches the rest of the modern Ground. It is a far cry from the small, spartan room for 50 with which the Club started out 200 years ago.

# Wellington or St John's

Today a spectator's likeliest approach to Lord's is a pleasant walk south from the art deco Tube station along Wellington Road to the North Gate, which is situated between the villas to the west, once owned by MCC, and the parade of London plane trees craning towards the cricket from the churchyard. But historically the main entrances to the Ground were on the south side along St John's Wood Road.

**W.G. Grace Gate at dawn before the First Test between England and West Indies. Photographed by Graham Morris, 6th May 2009**
Members do not have reserved seats in the Pavilion and so begin to queue from the early hours; Keith van Anderson is more often than not first in line.

*Mr Graham's Balloon at Lord's* by Robert Bremmel Schnebbelie (1839)
**British Museum Collection**
This watercolour, not previously published in the literature on Lord's, shows that entrance from James Dark's days, recalled by William Slatter as still standing in 1914.

From 1868 many visitors might have jumped off the Tube at a station at the "Coffin Corner" junction to the south-east of the Ground. From there the turnstiles and ticket windows of the East Gate would have been in sight. Originally known as St John's Wood Road, the station was named Lord's for a final few months before it closed in 1939, when today's station opened half a mile to the north.

The "Main Gate", a sliding wooden door behind the Mound, was by no means the entrance of choice. But it was replaced only in 1987 by the Bicentenary Gate, a handsome gift from the Duke of Westminster to celebrate the Club's double century and the memory of his father, an MCC President, Viscount Cobham.

By far the most popular way in, 50 yards to the west, was surely the double portal of the Lord's Hotel, later renamed the Tavern, which completed its century, but only just (1867–1967). Still mourned by many today, it had upheld the tradition first established by Thomas Lord himself, whose wine shop, set up to supply members and spectators, was the original entrance to the Ground. Its own traditions are upheld by cricket's most famous charity, founded on its sunny balcony: The Lord's Taverners, set up to support disabled and disadvantaged youngsters.

In 1919 it was decided to memorialise, in the words of Sir Stanley Jackson, "The Great Cricketer". The wrought-iron gates were supplied by the Bromsgrove Guild – makers of those at Buckingham Palace – and positioned at the south-western boundary. The Grace Gate is now the stately way to enter Lord's. Its symbol, the cricket ball with rising sun, was chosen by Sir Herbert Baker, creator of Father Time.

**Ceramic Tea Service by Lancaster and Sandland decorated with "Father Time" (1963)**
**Donated to MCC by the makers, 1963 and part acquired from the Keith Crump Collection, 2006**
The most recognisable feature of Lord's materialised in response to huge disappointment. The construction of a new Grandstand in 1926 caused no little consternation because so many seats had restricted viewing. Herbert Baker, the architect, felt forced to issue an apology. This took the form of a new weathervane to crown the new stand. Barring repairs and building work, it has swung above the Ground ever since. Its symbolism and derivation have caused much discussion, but the image has been adopted by organisations and clubs far beyond the boundaries of Lord's.

**Makhaya Ntini, photographed by Philip Brown, 2003**
The enduring appeal of playing at Lord's was never more evident than in the return of the South Africans in 1994. They won again in 1998 when they caused a stir with flag-waving on the visitors' balcony. In their third successive victory in 2003, Makhaya Ntini achieved the rare feat of ten wickets in the match and Graeme Smith compiled the highest ever innings by an overseas batsman at Lord's, 259, passing Sir Donald Bradman's 73-year-old record. It has not been a perennially happy hunting ground for cricket greats, though: Imran Khan, Brian Lara and Sachin Tendulkar have all performed below their best here.

THIS SPARROW WAS KILLED AT LORD'S BY A BALL
BOWLED BY JEHANGIR KHAN(CAMBRIDGE UNIVERSITY)
TO T. N. PEARCE(M.C.C.)
— ON JULY 3RD 1936.—

**Sparrow**
**Preserved by MCC**
**at the suggestion of**
**Col. Rait Kerr (1936)**
**Photographed by**
**Graham Morris, 2009**
An oasis in the heart of the city, Lord's has always been home to a variety of wildlife. Flying between batsman and bowler just after the point of delivery, this sparrow was struck a fatal blow by the ball from Jahangir Khan, playing for Cambridge in 1936. Perhaps the only animal to rival it was the black cat called Peter who actually achieved an obituary in *Wisden*: "Cat, Peter whose ninth life ended on Nov 5, 1964, was a well known cricket watcher at Lord's, where he spent 12 of his 14 years. He preferred a close-up view of proceedings and his sleek black form could often be seen prowling on the field of play when the crowds were the biggest ..."

*Leather Jacket C.C. Takes the Field* **by E.H. Shepard (1935)**
**Acquired by MCC from the Medici Gallery, 2012**
In 1935 an unusual combination of weather conditions provided the perfect environment for a "plague" of crane-fly (daddy-long-legs) larvae which fed on the roots of the grass outfield. Sir Pelham "Plum" Warner described the outfield as a "sea of sand". E.H. Shepard was born in St John's Wood, educated at the Royal Academy Schools and of course is most famous for his illustrations for the Pooh Bear books by A.A. Milne. He was a regular staff cartoonist for *Punch* from 1921 until 1953.

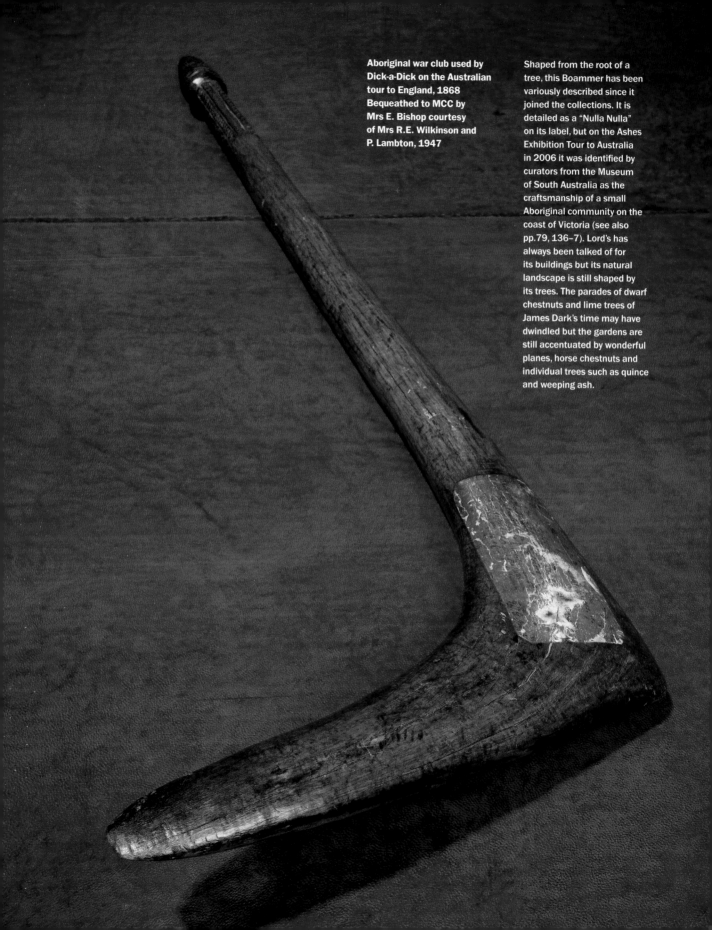

Aboriginal war club used by
Dick-a-Dick on the Australian
tour to England, 1868
Bequeathed to MCC by
Mrs E. Bishop courtesy
of Mrs R.E. Wilkinson and
P. Lambton, 1947

Shaped from the root of a
tree, this Boammer has been
variously described since it
joined the collections. It is
detailed as a "Nulla Nulla"
on its label, but on the Ashes
Exhibition Tour to Australia
in 2006 it was identified by
curators from the Museum
of South Australia as the
craftsmanship of a small
Aboriginal community on the
coast of Victoria (see also
pp.79, 136–7). Lord's has
always been talked of for
its buildings but its natural
landscape is still shaped by
its trees. The parades of dwarf
chestnuts and lime trees of
James Dark's time may have
dwindled but the gardens are
still accentuated by wonderful
planes, horse chestnuts and
individual trees such as quince
and weeping ash.

**Baggy Green caps worn by Don Bradman and Keith Miller, 1930 and 1948**
**Loaned from two private collections, 2003 and 2009**

It is no exaggeration to say that Keith Miller and Donald Bradman, two of the greatest Australian players to grace the Lord's turf, were like chalk and cheese. "The Don" burst onto the English scene in 1930, posting 254 – his favourite innings – at Lord's along with a triple century at Leeds and century at Trent Bridge. He continued to compile record after record and led the "Invincible" 1948 side of which Miller was such a charismatic part. Miller's relationship with Lord's never stopped growing and he was a hugely popular figure both in the commentary box and in the bars long after he stopped playing. A eucalyptus tree was planted on the coach mound in his memory.

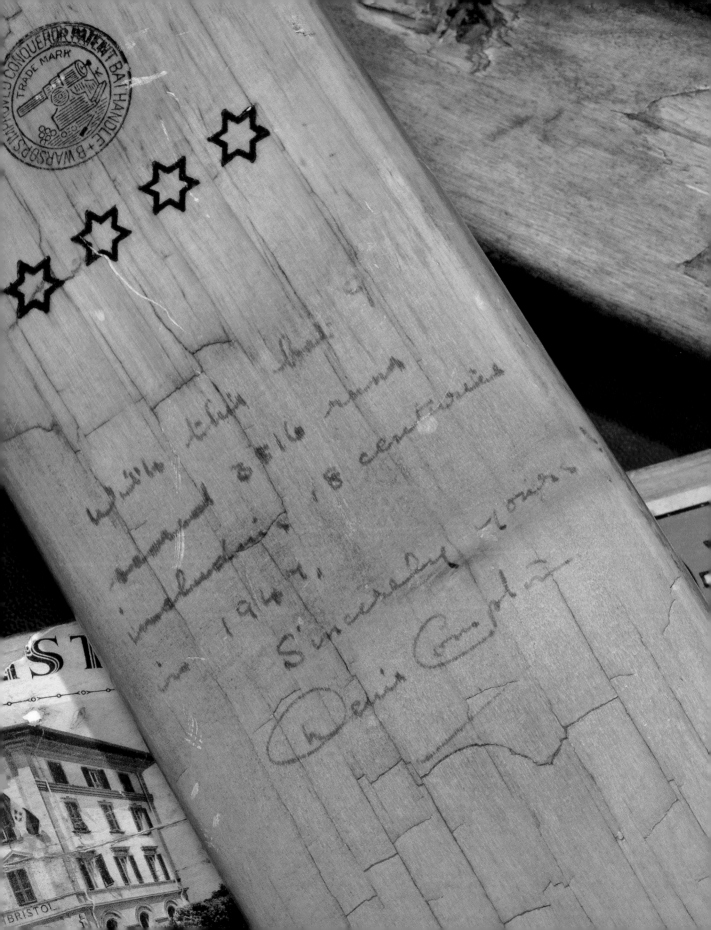

**Warsop bat used by
Denis Compton, 1947
Donated to MCC by B. Warsop
and D. Compton, 1956**

If Bradman and Miller
were arguably the greatest
Australian performers, it
would be hard not to rate
Denis Compton in the same
breath for England. His
summer of 1947 alongside
opening partner Bill Edrich is
still remembered reverently.
Compton's performances
seemed to hark directly back
to the golden pre-war days and
it was by common consent
that he and his partner were
memorialised in the new
stands built facing the Pavilion
in 1991. Writing to him to
solicit a donation for the
museum, MCC Curator Diana
Rait Kerr wished him a speedy
return to the team: "… The
English batting order without
you and Len would read rather
like Hamlet without the Prince
and Laertes."

**Wartime bats
Donated to MCC by
Mr A. Podmore and
Sir Ronald Ian Campbell,
KCMG, CB, 1917 and 1941**

Cricket sustained many through
the dark days of the two World
Wars. Sergeant J. Pigott
received a bat while fighting
in France in 1917; after this
first was damaged by shell fire,
another was duly requested
and sent. Sir Ronald Campbell,
UK envoy to Yugoslavia, was
interned with his staff near
Montepulciano after the fall of
Belgrade in 1941. He and his
fellow prisoners-of-war formed
the Chianciano "Cricket Club",
and signed this makeshift bat
in June that year, covering it
with labels from three local
*alberghi*.

**Bowlers' Bar bell**
**Cast by John Warner & Sons, 1884**
**Photographed by Matt Bright, 2008**

John Warner & Sons was founded as a firm in 1739 and continued under the same family ownership until it closed in 1949. Although all of its records were destroyed in the Blitz, it had foundries in various parts of London including Cheapside, Cripplegate, Spitalfields and Fleet Street. Warner's was the firm that accepted the original commission for Big Ben, though their sixteen-tonne bell cracked irreparably during testing in Old Westminster Yard. A recent innovation has been introduced at Lord's during Test Matches: each day the bell is rung by a visiting dignitary to signal the start of play. South African great Barry Richards enjoyed the honour during the 2008 Test.

**The Happy Warrior** by
**Frank Reynolds for** *Punch*
**magazine (1920)**
**Acquired by MCC from**
**Marina Warner, 2008**

There is arguably no name
more associated with Lord's,
Middlesex, the Ashes and
cricket than that of Sir Pelham
"Plum" Warner. Born in
Trinidad, he captained the
first tour organised by MCC
to Australia (see p.214),
entitling his travelogue
*How We Recovered the
Ashes*, which reignited the
association between the
Urn and cricket that had lain
dormant for twenty years.
In his last domestic season
he captained Middlesex to
the Championship before
managing the England team on
the infamous "Bodyline" tour.
He became President of MCC,
was eventually knighted and
was honoured at Lord's with his
own stand in 1958.

**Grandstand from the Visitors'
Dressing Room Balcony
Photographed by Richard
Green, 2012**

The Pavilion's middle balcony
is a relatively new addition and
allows leg-room akin to that
on a basic long-haul flight; it
results in a constant tattoo
of players' stud marks on the
railings. Michael Vaughan was
one of several players who
requested more comfortable
balcony benches, though he
did also ask to keep one of
those that were replaced. The
donations seen here from
Shane Warne, Makhaya Ntini
and Graeme Smith represent
their great moments at Lord's,
as do Graham Gooch's gloves
from his record innings of 333
(see also p.96).

**Binoculars
Donated to MCC by
Major F.D. Gillett, 1949**

The Committee Room is
perhaps the most hallowed
room at Lord's. The
governance of the domestic
and international game was
conducted around its heavy
Victorian oak tables for over
a century. On match days
it welcomes the monarch
and its rhythm is impeccably
maintained by a butler who
is of course an MCC Member.
Committee members and
guests may avail themselves
of binoculars gifted to the Club
by the Armed Services, or even
this mounted German anti-
aircraft Flakfernrohr, which
has been a fixture there
since 1949.

**We're Preparing it for Colin Cowdrey** by Patrick Blower, cartoon for the *Evening Standard* (2000)
**Acquired by MCC, 2001**
Many have sought to make Lord's their final resting place but permission has not always been forthcoming. The flint wall of the Harris Garden – so redolent of cricket's heartland in the Kentish weald – is the area where ashes may be scattered. Set off by climbing roses, soothed on summer match days by the sound of "Lyttelton" jazz, it is a happy and most English backdrop. It has always proved a natural gathering place, not just for match day crowds but also for touring teams arriving and departing and dignitaries at almost 100 years of ICC conferences.

**Graffiti on the balustrade of the Members' Bar, with the Mound Stand beyond** Photographed by Patrick Eagar, 2002
This balcony used to be the façade of the Players' Dressing Rooms, for incoming batsmen an unthinkable two floors up in the Pavilion. Its position surely indicates the unhurried pace of games gone by, and indeed it is clear that the 1902 Test provided the great Australians Warwick Armstrong and Victor Trumper with plenty of time to etch themselves into the Lord's fabric (rain allowed only 38 overs). Michael Hopkins, architect of the acclaimed Mound Stand, took inspiration from the canopied roof over those early Dressing Rooms in designing his own tented pavilion; his goal was to ensure a relaxed atmosphere in which people felt at ease for a day's spectating.

" WE'RE PREPARING IT FOR COLIN COWDREY "

THE GAMES
OF
LAWN TENNIS
AND
BADMINTON

M. C. C.

**Lawn Tennis and Badminton: Laws of the Game Drafted by MCC, 1878**

In 1838 it was decided to add a real tennis court to the facilities at Lord's. Since that time there has always been an area of the Ground dedicated to tennis, racquets or squash. What is less well known is that MCC drew up one of the earliest sets of rules for lawn tennis and maintained grass courts on the outfield, in the north-east corner of the Ground and finally in the Harris Garden. In recent years the Club was approached unsuccessfully to hold a pre-Wimbledon grass court tournament, inviting the delightful prospect of the men at Queen's and women at Lord's.

*Practising at the Nets, Lord's by Arthur Hopkins for the Daily Graphic (c.1910)*
**Acquired by MCC, before 1907**

The Nursery Ground is a feature not replicated at any other Test ground and sustains the long association between Lord's Grounds, pleasure gardens and market gardens. It really was made up of fruit and vegetable nurseries; Guy's was purchased in 1869 and the more famous 3½-acre Henderson's, renowned for its tulips and pineapples, was acquired in the Club's centenary year 1887 for £18,500. It was sold by the Clergy Orphan School, whose land also became a part of Lord's less than five years later; happily its legacy lives on in the education and net-training of young cricketers that coincidentally chimes with the truth behind the "Nursery" Ground.

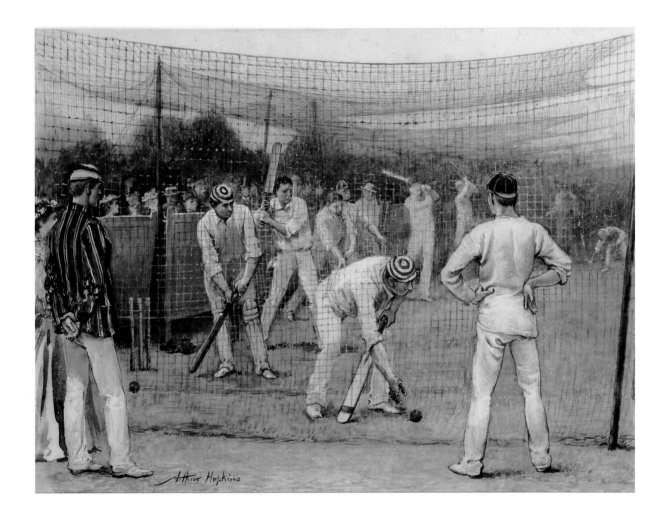

# Home from Home

Lord's is England's Ground, but it has been home to Middlesex players since 1877. A portrait of R.D. Walker, scion of the founding family, hangs in the Pavilion, and famous captains – Warner and Allen – survey the Committee Room, where Mikes Brearley and Gatting can often still be found helping to shape the game. Though Clive Radley has just retired as coach at the Academy, Angus Fraser and Mark Ramprakash now mentor the latest Middlesex and England stars Steve Finn and Eoin Morgan.

Andrew Strauss with Lord's branding alongside the Nursery Ground Nets
Photographed by Sarah Williams

### Andrew Strauss at Home

Andrew Strauss first set eyes on the Ground when he came to watch the Test in which Graham Gooch compiled the highest innings ever scored at Lord's.

"Needless to say, I was impressed."

His next visit, trialling for the Middlesex 2nd XI in a net session on the Nursery, gave him a taste of things to come and one that he says just doesn't go away. "However often you come here, you can never be blasé; this Ground always manages to retain its special character."

Did that extend to the dressing room? "Sure, you have your own spot, your locker to store your kit. When I arrived I couldn't believe that there was a seat next to Justin Langer. What I didn't understand was that he wasn't the most even-tempered guy. After a bad innings, he threw his bat, his helmet … there was always collateral damage!"

How does he view things now that he has put his playing days behind him? "Well, it will be a chance to get to know the rest of the Ground – the gardens to which my friends come religiously year after year, doing the same thing, meeting the same people. Maybe I'll see a little more of the Media Centre, from the inside … One thing's for sure, when I retired I realised that that seat in the dressing room wasn't mine; I was just looking after it for a while and now I've passed it on."

**Andrew Strauss reaches his hundred on his Test debut against New Zealand, Lord's, 21st May 2004 Photographed by Patrick Eagar**

# 3.
# Cutting the Mustard

I often heard it said at Christie's that collectors each have a flaw, lack a certain something which gives them the impetus to collect. Their collections gradually take on a life of their own, inherit a DNA that reflects this. In the case of the MCC collection this DNA does not reflect a single collector but its many contributors; the collection complements the great playing traditions of Lord's with a rich sense of Club ritual and underpins their history by its physical presence. It literally provides the material basis for the claim by Lord's to be the home of the game.

The collection today is universally acclaimed and stands favourable comparison with those of its peers, the Royal Company of Archers, the Royal and Ancient Golf Club of St Andrews and the Jockey Club. As at those other ancient sites, those at Lord's initially decorated their clubhouse. The Honorary Secretary George Aislabie (1822–42) not only donated a snuff box for the Club Room but left three portraits and an imposing marble bust commissioned by subscription from Edward Davis; William Slatter recalled Aislabie lying on a table in that same Club room while his father helped to prepare the plaster mould for that very bust.

The incidental furniture and fixtures, priced at around £1500, that were included with the leasehold comprised a number of portraits including the great players of the day: Alfred Mynn, George Parr, John Wisden (see pp.224, 228) and James Dean among others. They were painted by Walter Bromley III, grandson of the famous engraver of the same name who had worked locally for the great artist Edwin Landseer. These in all likelihood were commissioned by James Dark, tenant at Lord's from the 1830s. Bromley was married to Dark's niece and lived in an adjoining "white house" (as they were known) on St John's Wood Road.

As the Club set to developing the Ground, so the Treasurer Sir Spencer Ponsonby-Fane set himself the task of adding to this meagre inheritance of pictures. He sought out portraits of all the recognised Presidents of MCC to bolster the Club's history. By 1912 he had succeeded in his aim, giving preference to a list of over 80 such items in his catalogue. These were photographs, engravings and in some cases original drawings presented by the sitters themselves or their relatives. From his initiative, Presidential portraits have continuously hung at Lord's for over a century and the photgraphic collection has grown threefold.

**MCC Committee Minute book (1928), with details of the donation of the Ashes Urn by Florence, Lady Darnley**

### Minutes of the Committee Meeting.

Present — At a meeting of the Committee held at Lord's, on Monday, July 2nd, 1928 at 4.30 p.m. Present :—The President (in the chair), Earl of Dartmouth, Lord Hawke, Mr. A. J. Webbe, Earl Howe, Sir Francis E. Lacey, Lieut.-Col. F. H. Browning, Lieut.-Col. C. Heseltine, Mr. F. H. Hollins, Lord Leconfield, Captain R. T. Stanyforth and Mr. W. H. Patterson by invitation.

Minutes — The minutes of the last meeting as printed and circulated were signed as correct.

The Finance Sub-Committee reported :—

Club Balances — 1. That the club balances on current account were at Glyn's £1,363. 13s. 10d. at Barclays £1,264. 3s. 1d. total £2,627. 16s. 11d.

M.C.C. v. Holland — 2. That it was necessary to make travelling arrangements for the M.C.C. team which will visit Holland at the end of the month and that the inclusive cost of the fares, etc., would be £70. 16s. 0d. (It was agreed that the Club should forward a cheque to Messrs. T. Cook & Son for this amount, the money to be recovered from the members of the team.)

The Secretary reported:—

The Urn containing the Ashes, Presentation of — 1. That the Dowager Countess of Darnley had forwarded to M.C.C. the urn containing the ashes of Anglo-Australian Cricket. (It was decided to ask Lady Darnley if she would be able to make the presentation in person.)

M.C.C. Tour in Australia — 2. That a reply had been received from the Australian Board of Control in regard to the playing conditions and financial arrangements for the M.C.C. Australian tour. (It was decided to ask the Australian Board of Control to consider further the practicability of eliminating the matches at Bathurst and Goulburn but it was not thought necessary to press for increased guarantees at Brisbane and in Tasmania.)

No. 8, Elm Tree Road — 3. That a letter had been received from the Club's agents in regard to letting No. 8, Elm Tree Road. (Deferred.)

Gentlemen v. Players — 4. That as the Test Match at Manchester immediately follows Gentlemen v. Players at Lord's it would be necessary to alter the usual hours of play in the Gentlemen v. Players match. (It was decided that the hours of play should be 11.30 to 6.30 first and second days, 11 to 5.30 third day.)

Mr. R. G. Warner presents photograph — 5. That Mr. R. G. Warner had offered to present to the Club a photograph of Lord's Pavilion, 1881. (Thanks.)

West Indies' Test Match — 6. That Captain A. Vickerman, a member of the Club, had not received his Test Match tickets for which he had paid 12/-. (It was decided to refund this sum to Captain Vickerman.)

Arrangements at Lord's Test Match — 7. That Mr. G. N. E. Hall-Say had writtten in regard to (a) admission of members to the ground (b) pass-out checks (c) autograph hunters (d) a Royal box.

M.C.C. in Holland — 8. That on the occasion of the M.C.C. tour in Holland the Hague Cricket Club would celebrate its Jubilee and that the Committee might care to forward a letter of congratulation. (Approved.)

Property abutting on Lord's — 9. That Messrs. Smith, Oakley and Garrard's valuation of certain property abutting on Lord's had been received. (Consideration of this matter was deferred pending further enquiries.)

Grand Stand Hot Water arrangements — 10. That no provision had been made for the supply of boiling water for tea in the boxes in the new Grand Stand. (No action at present.)

His energy and enthusiasm was key to the establishment of a tradition of collecting and in encouraging others to donate. His accession to the office of Treasurer was crucial too, enabling a fair financial wind from the Club for further purchases. That said, when he began he picked up items for as little as a few pence, and felt somewhat cheated as the price rose in response to his demand.

Those were the days of the two great touring sides, the United England XI and the All-England XI. As fate would have it, Nicolas "Felix" Wanostracht was both a player and an artist. Many original watercolour portraits by him, including that of Sir Spencer, now hang at Lord's alongside two sketchbooks that form an illustrated travelogue of the exploits and venues of William Clarke's ground-breaking All-England XI (see p.138). Felix's work did not come directly to the Club, although the great Victorian artist G.F. Watts, his neighbour, did give the Club five balletic drawings from which the illustrations to the renowned book *Felix on the Bat* were taken. Felix himself is thought to be the model for these, although Sir Spencer believed his brother Frederick Ponsonby modelled for "Leg cut". More Watts drawings were purchased just a few years later, showing a partiality for works by the great Victorian artist.

Mementos of the great players of the age were also collected. The selection of personal items belonging to the great W.G. includes belt and boots, bats and caps, snuffbox and silver kettle, travelling bag and doorplate; the manuscripts of his book *Cricket* were given by his publisher, and a plaster bust by his widow. In most cases, items were donated and only in special cases was a purchase considered. Families of the great Victor Trumper, R.E. Foster, Wilfred Rhodes, C.K. Nayudu, Bert Oldfield, Jim Laker and David Sheppard have all continued this tradition, which has resulted in a collection large enough to trace the developments, fashion, techniques and innovations of the game through the personal writings, belongings and images of the finest players of all three centuries.

Alongside these collections sit more singular objects, and none more so than the Ashes Urn. We are not sure what it was, nor what is in it; we did not know until 75 years after it was donated that it was broken, and we have only just pieced together its early history. It stands just 4½ inches tall, yet it resonates with rivalry, friendship and memories for more sports fans than any other object.

Another gift of Australian origin and uncertain provenance is that of the Aboriginal Boammer (p.62). Brought on tour by Dick-a-Dick, one of the 1868 Australian tourists, it was sent to MCC by a Mrs Wilkinson for safekeeping in 1947. Enquiries elicited that it had been "removed" by a military unit from a house in Croydon after it was requisitioned in 1941. Correspondence with the house's previous owner could only confirm its "use for fratricidal purposes" by her sons!

A further flurry of donations was made in the lead-up to the Second World War. Many were made by military members of MCC, of whom there were and remain many. In some cases these were souvenirs such as the German anti-flak binoculars that stand sentry in the Committee Room (p.69); in others they were items of cricketing importance sent for safekeeping. As it was, the MCC collection had itself been sent away from Lord's for its own safety. Some of the pictures still bear the address labels of the country rectory to which they were sent.

The result was that by the end of the war the collection had outgrown the Pavilion and the small share of Captain Carlton Levick's time that could be devoted to it. The Secretary wrote a memorandum to the Committee summarising the challenge facing the Club in this respect. The result was a momentous decision not only to employ a full-time Curator but also to create a dedicated gallery. The choice of Diana Rait Kerr, the Secretary's daughter, might well be looked at askance from the distance of a generation or three, but unsurprisingly, given her father's skills and interests (he was an acknowledged expert on the Laws of the Game), the appointment was a resounding success.

The collections received a new dynamism and focus. In redecorating the Pavilion, the Arts and Library Committee were directed to *Wisden* and decided that the Cricketers of the Year award would form the perfect criteria for pictorial displays. At the same time, it was confirmed that a memorial gallery would be the ideal way to mark the recent sacrifice of the many cricketers from all countries who had given their lives in conflict. These two ideas combined at almost the same time as the Baseball Museum and Hall of Fame in Cooperstown, New York was founded. Geoffrey Moorhouse, no natural friend to Lord's, much admired the American museum but thought Lord's "far better served by not having something as monotonous and ridiculously obsequious as the Hall of Fame itself". The Memorial Gallery precluded this.

With a dedicated home for the existing holdings, Miss Rait Kerr set out to ensure that the collections were kept up to date and of the highest quality. She

*The Cut* by G.F. Watts (c.1837)
**Original drawing from a series of five for *Felix on the Bat***
**Donated to MCC by the artist, 1895**
This drawing was dedicated to William Ward, a fine cricketer, governor of the Bank of England and the man responsible for securing the future of the Ground from Thomas Lord in 1825.

wrote to the greats such as Jack Hobbs, Len Hutton and Denis Compton to ask them to donate; she was charming, steadfast and not to be denied.

Not satisfied with this, she embarked on a series of exhibitions both at home and abroad that included a display within the Festival of Britain. In all her efforts she was supported by an indefatigable Harry Altham, Treasurer 1949–63, about whom I have not heard a bad word spoken. Blended with his commitment to youth cricket was a love of the history of the game and he used his personal contacts and those of the Club to elicit further donations from great collectors such as his friend Evelyn Rockley Wilson.

The 1970s seem to have been something of a quiet time for collecting. Altham had died and was himself memorialised in the museum in 1965, and Diana Rait Kerr had handed over to her successor Stephen Green in 1968. Perhaps too it was a result of MCC's involvement in upheavals in the cricketing world: the handing over of the reins of domestic cricket to the TCCB, and the devastating effects of the mass defection to World Series Cricket at the behest of Kerry Packer and Tony Greig. It was early in the next decade that attention focused on the collections once again. However, this time it was the work of researchers that prompted a most unexpected and delicate problem for the new Curator.

On 21st August 1983 the *Mail on Sunday* published a feature entitled "Revealed: The MCC Fake Art Treasures". The article alleged that over a third of the paintings hanging in the Memorial Gallery were not authentic. Robin Simon had been curating an exhibition of cricket art with Alastair Smart, and as the exhibition went on display at York City Art Gallery this news broke.

Naturally MCC were taken aback and found themselves in a particularly sensitive situation given that the large proportion of these pictures had been donated by the Colman family – of mustard fame. Sir Jeremiah Colman I had been an avid collector and had been readily supplied by distinguished dealers during the 1920s and 1930s. He had made the initial donation in 1947 and the paintings had been hung as a group in response to his request. A second bequest

*Bidding was simple …*
**by Barry Fantoni**
**Pen and ink cartoon, probably for *The Times* (1987)**
The artist trained at the Slade School before cartooning for *Private Eye* and later joining their editorial staff. He created a "Hall of Fame" series with the express intention of "chopping people down to size".

*I always thought it was a fake …*
**Lithograph by JAK (1983)**
The caption continues:
"It's nothing like Boycott's stance at the crease!"

of the bulk of the collection, by his son Jeremiah II, was made shortly afterwards, bringing the gift to 50 paintings.

A report to the MCC Committee two days later outlined the situation and confirmed the likelihood of fakes within the collection. Diana Rait Kerr made it clear that she had had suspicions from the time the collection was accepted and that even her display labels bore this out. E.W. Swanton's letter to *The Times* made clear that MCC's displays did not attempt "to replicate the Tate Gallery".

Despite this bluff, a working party was swiftly convened taking advantage of the offer of assistance by Messrs Sotheby & Co. with their conservator and the generous offer by Sir Jeremiah's grandson of £1,000 to allay the necessary expenses. The report was stark: as of 16th October, of the 39 pictures the group had examined, 27 were not genuine. In their opinion there was a common hand which had added a contrived cricket scene to what were genuine landscapes in authentic frames. To make matters worse, there were some tell-tale characteristics to both the style of painting and the "documentary" backing labels which, by basic scrutiny, might have roused suspicion.

The pictures were swiftly re-arranged and re-described – and removed completely from the Long Room – while one of the dealers issued a writ against the newspaper that implied they sold to Sir Jeremiah under false pretences. This suit continued into the summer of 1984 until a final apology was issued by the paper. MCC quietly handed back over twenty paintings to the Colmans, requesting just two things: to retain one fake picture and to avoid further publicity.

The Club's Bicentenary seems nevertheless to have provided enough encouragement to celebrate its history and cultivate the richness of its annals once again. This it did in two completely contrasting ways. The first was to conjure up ghosts of the past by creating a set of honours boards to celebrate great performances at Lord's. This idea was so inspired that now it seems to be the aim of all international players to make their mark at Lord's. Jonty Rhodes was the first to tape up his name immediately after scoring a century and this gesture turned into a trend which still continues, to the extent that in 2009 Ravi Bopara signalled to the Dressing Room to do the same before his innings was even over.

The second "celebration" was the auction of almost 850 items, including bats, balls, clothing, handkerchiefs, portraits, cartoons and prints. Tim Rice in his book *Treasures at Lord's* describes the decision as giving a new lease of life to forgotten or duplicate gems "languishing" at Lord's. That such sales may sometimes prove necessary, I must admit; that every effort was made to seek permission from the donors was good practice; but the sale of unique items that illustrate important themes in cricket's development was perhaps a little ill-judged. Happily, many of the important items are now displayed in the Melbourne Cricket Club's museum where the Australian public and  many English visitors will be able still to view them.

It is gratifying that the funds raised were committed to new commissions and acquisitions, and the Club, increasingly aware of their importance and appeal to a wider public, whether significant individual items or more generic collections, has redoubled its efforts to exhibit and lend whenever possible.

# Elders and Betters

In the Dressing Room at Lord's, the great names of the game silently send down their challenge from the honours boards. Barrington, Hutton and Hammond all averaged over 50 in Tests, Gooch scored the highest individual innings at the Ground and Ian Botham holds the Test wicket tally. Yet that challenge has been taken up by a new generation: Alastair Cook has now recorded more centuries than any other Englishman and Jimmy Anderson has recently become England's all-time wicket taker in all international formats.

**Chris Broad's jacket for Ashes Tour to Australia, 1986–7 Stuart Broad's England uniform worn at Lord's, 2011–12** Father and son have both performed outstandingly for England in Ashes series. Stuart is the only Englishman other than Ian Botham to have both scored a century and taken a ten-wicket haul in a Lord's Test.

## The Family History
Nick Compton

Growing up in sport-mad South Africa meant every weekend was taken up by cricket, rugby, soccer and tennis. At that age I was of course aware of my grandfather's prowess, but being in South Africa and being young my passion was to fulfil my own talent.

Cricket became my number one sport when I went to high school. I excelled and knew then that this was what I wanted to be. I don't honestly think any conscious thought of my grandfather ever came into it, but I'm sure the genes had something to do with nurturing my love and ambition for the game.

It's been a long road getting here, and as I went through the ranks in England I became more aware of Denis's amazing stats, but more importantly the impact he had on people at a tough time in post-war Britain. He was more than just a sportsman, he was an entertainer and a man for the people. I just feel enormously proud to share the family history. Hopefully I can make my own bit of history but I will have to do it in my own way of course.

Playing and winning in India is not something many people can boast about. To be a part of the team there in 2012 was one thing but to be batting when we won two historic Test Matches, trust me, is something I will hold close to me. It makes me very ambitious to keep producing, to keep playing, because I know that if I can with this team there will be a lot more similar feelings.

**Pen and ink cartoon by SAK (1927)**
In 1927, returning to cricket after serious illness, Walter Hammond made an immediate impact, becoming only the second man to score 1000 runs in the first month of the cricket season.

**Helmets worn by Sunil Gavaskar and Brian Lara, 1987 and 1994**
**Donated to MCC in 1987 and acquired at auction, 2006**
Sunny Gavaskar held world records for the most Test runs and Test centuries and finally scored a century at Lord's in the Bicentenary match, in his last first-class match. He wore this, one of the early style of helmets, in the match. Brian Lara was a later holder of the Test runs record; he also scored the highest individual score in a Test innings, 400 not out, and the highest individual score in first-class cricket, 501 not out for Warwickshire. In the latter innings he batted in this helmet, borrowed from David Fulton as his own had been hit full on by a delivery in the previous game.

**Memorabilia from the Golden Age: Victor Trumper, Wilfred Rhodes, R.E. Foster, Gilbert Jessop**
**Loaned and donated to MCC, 1940s–1980s**
No one who saw him play argued there was another to match the stylish genius of Victor Trumper, widely mourned at the age of only 37. Caps, blazer and pads, donated by his wife among others, were complemented by a bat of 1905 (from Colonel Rex Osborne) inscribed: "This which I selected at the beginning of our tour is the best that I have ever used and never want a better." The relatives of the great R.E. Foster, who died aged 36, also donated his bat from 1903–4. His innings of 287 not out in Sydney remains an Ashes record on debut.

**Claire Taylor**
**Photographed by**
**Graham Morris, 2010**
Claire Taylor is rightly lauded as the finest batsman of her generation and arguably the finest ever to represent England Women. She holds the record for the highest One-Day International score at Lord's, 156 not out, has won both the ICC Women's World Cup and ICC Women's World Twenty20 and was celebrated by *Wisden* as the first female Cricketer of the Year (see pp.100–01) in 2010. When the award was announced she was photographed in the Long Room with one of Andrew Festing's paintings, a conversation piece depicting England cricketers from the 1970s and 1980s. MCC has recently commissioned a portrait to honour her contribution to cricket.

***Jack Hobbs* by Tom Webster (c.1925)**
**Acquired by MCC,**
**date unknown**

Jack Hobbs has no peer in English cricket and was selected as one of *Wisden*'s five Cricketers of the Century. His prodigious batting garnered him over 60,000 first-class runs and one short of 200 first-class centuries. Little wonder he was known as "The Master". Although he was a renowned Surrey player, MCC has a wealth of material relating to his career including items he himself donated. His record for the highest individual score at Lord's (316 not out for Surrey against Middlesex in 1926) was only surpassed in 1990 by Graham Gooch (see pp.68, 96). Tom Webster taught himself to draw while he worked in a railway booking office. He joined the *Mail* in 1919 and worked there for over twenty years specialising in sporting cartoons. At his peak, the paper placed placards at sporting events to announce his presence and one journalist said he excited more interest at a sporting gathering than all bar the Prince of Wales.

:AFTER MAKING 22 ONLY. THAT BAT FOLLOWS JACK HOBBS INTO THE PAVILION BEGGING FOR ANOTHER CHANCE:

[BY TOM WEBSTER:]

**CBE and Knighthood awarded to Sir Alec Bedser in 1982 and 1996**

**Bequeathed to MCC, 2010**

In a first-class career lasting 21 years Sir Alec Bedser took 1924 wickets for Surrey (who dominated county cricket for a decade), MCC and England at an average of 20.41, including 236 at 24.89 in 51 Tests. Don Bradman fell more times in Tests to Bedser than to anyone else, and at Adelaide in 1946–7 he described his dismissal by Bedser as the best ball he ever faced. From 1969 to 1981, Sir Alec served as Chairman of Selectors for the England team. Along with his twin brother Eric, from whom he was famously inseparable, he remained a regular visitor to Lord's right up to his death in 2010.

**The President's "Chair"
Commissioned by MCC,
date unknown**

This unusual piece of furniture holds images of all the MCC Presidents to have held the post from the time of the destruction of the earliest Pavilion in 1825. It sits in a prominent position outside the Committee Room, opposite the Presidential honours boards, and the Committee Dining Room is now decorated with its portraits. The gift of the Presidency lies with the current holder who traditionally, taking advice from a select few, then designates his successor at the AGM in early May. In one stretch of sixteen years, fourteen Presidents were related by marriage. The first professional cricketer to be appointed was Tom Graveney in 2004.

| Year | Name | Country | |
|---|---|---|---|
| | ...DSLEY | | |
| | M. MACARTNEY | AUSTRALIA | |
| | D. G. BRADMAN | AUSTRALIA | |
| | W. M. WOODFULL | AUSTRALIA | |
| ...34 | C. S. DEMPSTER | AUSTRALIA | |
| 1935 | M. L. PAGE | AUSTRALIA | |
| 1938 | W. A. BROWN | SOUTH AFRICA | |
| | B. MITCHELL | AUSTRALIA | |
| 1939 | W. A. BROWN | AUSTRALIA | |
| | D. G. BRADMAN | AUSTRALIA | |
| | G. A. HEADLEY | NEW ZEALAND | |
| 1947 | G. A. HEADLEY | NEW ZEALAND | |
| 1948 | A. MELVILLE | AUSTRALIA | |
| | A. R. MORRIS | SOUTH AFRICA | |
| 1949 | S. G. BARNES | AUSTRALIA | |
| | M. P. DONNELLY | AUSTRALIA | |
| | A. F. RAE | WEST INDIES | |
| | C. L. WALCOTT | WEST INDIES | |
| | M. H. MANKAD | SOUTH AFRICA | |
| | L. HASSETT | AUSTRALIA | |
| | MILLER | AUSTRALIA | |
| | ...CLEAN | NEW ZEALAND | |
| | ...RY | WEST INDIES | |
| | | WEST INDIES | |
| | | INDIA | |

**Lord's honours boards
Commissioned by MCC,
1986–7**

A relatively recent addition to the Dressing Rooms, the honours boards have captured the imagination of visitors and spurred the ambition of players. They are modest in appearance and styling and match the utilitarian atmosphere of the Dressing Rooms that has only occasionally been punctuated by decoration or photographs. Only one man features on the boards in both Dressing Rooms: Gordon Greenidge scored two centuries for West Indies at Lord's, but he also appeared for MCC in the Bicentenary match, and his century in that game was recognised – an anomaly, some would say – among the England Test innings in the Home Dressing Room.

***The Majesty of Empire:
G. Headley Leaving the Pavilion
by James Thorpe (1933)
Donated to MCC by
R.S. McMinn, 1949***

George Headley made his debut for West Indies in 1930, shortly after they were admitted to Test cricket. He was their star batsman – appearing more than once as a centurion at Lord's – and averaged over 60, albeit in a relatively short career by today's standards. Inevitably this was due to the Second World War, but he did succeed in becoming the first black captain of the side in 1948 and both his son and grandson played Test cricket (for West Indies and England respectively). This cartoon by James Thorpe captures the pressure on a player coming out to bat at Lord's.

THE MAJESTY OF EMPIRE
Headley leaving the pavilion

Lord's has seen many fine bowling performances over the years but the feat of taking ten wickets in a match is as rare as the proverbial hen's teeth. Bob Massie famously achieved this in his debut test for Australia against England but never really captured the same form hat-trick in his debut here for South Africa (see p.164). Jim Laker took fifteen wickets for Surrey against MCC but more importantly he is represented by his wife's donation of the balls with which he achieved the unsurpassed record of nineteen wickets in a Test Match at Old Trafford in 1956.

**England record bats used by Graham Gooch, Rob Key, Andrew Flintoff and Matt Prior Donated or loaned by the players, 1990–2012**

Lord's has not always proved a happy hunting ground for England; the view from the home Dressing Room has often been one of trepidation. However these bats attest to some exhilarating innings by Englishmen. Graham Gooch's record achievement in scoring 333 against India in 1990 was pictured on his bat by Jack Russell. Andrew Flintoff's bat failed to sustain his explosive power, splitting apart in his 142 against South Africa in 2003, while the unblemished surface of Rob Key's bat pays insufficient tribute to his maiden Test century (221 in fact) against the West Indies in 2004. Matt Prior became the first England wicketkeeper to score a hundred on debut at Lord's in 2007.

**Sir Viv Richards batting at Lord's Photographed by Patrick Eagar, 1988**

Viv Richards is pictured here batting at the height of his powers. He still holds the highest score in a One-Day International at Lord's (138 not out) as well as appearing on the honours boards with a Test century. The unmistakable windows of the Pavilion form a perfect background in this backlit image by Patrick Eagar, the renowned photographer who covered over 50 Test Matches at the Ground. It has not always been easy to photograph at Lord's but Patrick knows it better than anyone: 11am on a summer morning, for example, is when the Pavilion is at its finest, just as the sunshine hits the terracotta façade with full force.

**Fred Trueman by
Lawrence Toynbee
Donated to MCC by Lord
Hutchinson in memory of
Alan Ross, 2006**

This drawing captures
unmistakeably the action of
(so stated *Wisden*) probably
the greatest of England's truly
fast bowlers. Fred went further,
only half-jokingly calling himself
"the greatest that ever drew
breath". His fellow Yorkshire
bowler Bill Bowes described
him as having the perfect
combination: a love of bowling
fast, a powerful physique and
a smooth cartwheel action,
and he went on to become
the first man to take 300 Test
wickets, at an average only just
above 20.

**Cricket Writers' Club Young
Player of the Year Trophy
Loaned to MCC, 2010**

The Cricket Writers' Club
is open to recognised
correspondents of newspapers
and periodicals and those
involved in radio and television.
Taking inspiration from the
Empire CWC set up in 1946–7
to fill a fortnight's delay before
the first fixture of the MCC
Tour to Australia, it set out to
promote and play cricket. It
is now represented at Lord's
in the list of its Presidents in
the J.P. Morgan Media Centre.
At the end of season dinner
they traditionally award a
number of prizes. One of these
is the Peter Smith Award for
outstanding contribution to
cricket; Peter was a noted
correspondent and, at the
persistent urging of CWC,
became the first official Press
Officer at Lord's.

# Cricketers of the Year

Cricket has no need for a contrived or retrospective Hall of Fame. Chosen at the time by the editor of cricket's "bible", the *Wisden* Cricketers of the Year have been selected annually since 1889. A reflection of their imperfect times (the war years bear no names), they nonetheless capture the range and breadth of cricket in England from the county stalwart and public schoolboy to the international star and best female player: an irresistible combination around which to collect cricket's history.

**Andy Flower, Zimbabwe**
**Test Cap**
**Donated to MCC 2012**
**Portrait of Andy Flower by**
**Jennifer McRae (detail)**
**Commissioned by MCC, 2009**
Flower was named *Wisden*
Cricketer of the Year in 2002

## My Cap
Andy Flower

When I made my Test debut, in 1992 versus India at Harare Sports Club, we had a team dinner in the old colonial pavilion overlooking the field on the eve of the match.

Speeches were made, the odd beer calmed the inevitable nerves. No caps were handed out. The caps we were using at the time were cheap baseball caps, already in use at training!

It was only later in my career, when some enlightened captain or coach insisted on the Zimbabwe Cricket Union sourcing the genuine article, that we were presented with the Zimbabwean version of the Baggy Green – exact replicas of the Baggy Green, made by the same company in Australia, but embroidered with The Zimbabwe Bird, the country's national emblem.

Through my Test career I only wore that one cap. The Bird is faded and the green is stained white with the sweat of many overs of toil, mostly from behind the stumps on long days in the field. In my mind that cap is a symbol of the effort we put in to make our country proud, to justify our Test status, and to see just how good we could be in the elevated world of international cricket.

I've donated it to Lord's. It seems to me to be a symbol of the link between my personal history with my country, Zimbabwe, and the new life that I and my family have been lucky enough to be welcomed into in England. The MCC has been a big part of that welcome. So thank you.

**Eoin Morgan
Photographed in the Long
Room by Clare Skinner**
Morgan was *Wisden* Cricketer
of the Year 2011

# 4.
# It's the Taking Part

In the winter 2011 issue of MCC's magazine, Howard Hanley's research into the signatures etched on the balcony rail of the early Dressing Rooms picked out the initials or nicknames of a number of the most famous Australians of the early 1900s: Trumble, Trumper and Armstrong, to name but three (see p.71). Alongside them survives the simple memorial "E. Reeve 1903". Research into his record suggests a more modest level of achievement. He played at Lord's once for the London Playing Fields Association against MCC. He was nought not out in the first innings, did not bat in the second, did not bowl and took no catches. Still, it's the taking part that matters, and his name does sit in illustrious company.

This sense of contributing in some way to the history of Lord's is a strong one, and, though Reeve is an extreme example, the essence of the Ground is that wonderful combination of individual and group effort, not just out on the field of play but in all the associated roles and occupations that enable cricket to take place.

Patronage was of the utmost importance to the popularity of the early game; it was encouraged by the huge amounts of money to be won by the wealthy nobles who, with the fillip of royal favour, created the fashion for gambling on cricket. The very richest aristocrats teamed up with the best players from the lower classes, often hired as their staff, giving rise to the apocryphal claim that if their French peers had played cricket with their serfs there would have been no Revolution.

The first overseas tours were primarily driven by commercial considerations and backed by prominent individuals and interested parties in both countries. So the first England side to Australia was backed by caterers Spiers & Pond, and Ivo Bligh's XI of 1882–3 by Lord Clarke from Melbourne. Some of the professional players played in and promoted the tours, but without the support of significant amateurs were often financially disappointed (see p.142).

In 1888–9 Major Wharton's XI was the first to tour South Africa. It was organised by an army officer who had been stationed in the Cape since 1883 and was a member of the Western Province Cricket Club. The side was captained by Charles Aubrey Smith and played some terrifically entertaining cricket in response to an enthusiastic welcome. In fact, in Kimberly, the visitors were said to have been entertained far into the night and gone straight out to play without heading to bed. *Wisden*, however, reported that the tour did not cover its expenses, although the backers had secured Cecil Rhodes to underwrite it. Furthermore Sir Donald Currie, owner of the Castle Shipping Line (*SS Garth Castle*) with whom they travelled, donated a cup to be presented to the team who performed best against the visitors (Kimberly, as it turned out!), and it subsequently became the domestic trophy for South African cricket. He did the same a year later for the first English rugby team to tour.

Previous pages: Celebratory lunch for the Duke of Edinburgh's 90th birthday in the Long Room, 2012. Photographed by Matt Bright. The Duke is Patron of over a hundred sports organisations and charities and has twice been president of MCC.

Aubrey Smith stayed on in Johannesburg to work but later became well known for his acting career, and his moustachioed portrait (lent through the auspices of the Lord's announcer, Johnny Dennis) can be seen in the Pavilion, as can a study, drawn (in 1948) and donated by John Gilroy (1955). He is perhaps best known in cricketing circles for founding the Hollywood Cricket Club, 43 years after his appearances in South Africa. He was an indomitable character and started a resurgence of cricketing interest in California with his strict adherence to the traditions of coloured blazers (taken from the Thespids club in London), punctuality and decorum. As David Niven recalled, "When that Grand Old Man asked you to play, you played." When Laurence Olivier arrived in 1933 to begin work as a film star in America, a note awaited him at the Chateau Marmont Hotel: "There will be nets tomorrow at 9am. I trust I shall see you there." The club established itself in Griffith Park with an impressive pavilion and outfield seeded with grass imported from England. It even toured Canada in 1936 with Nigel Bruce and Errol Flynn among their number, and memorabilia and records of both tour and Club, held at the C.C. Morris Cricket Library in Haverford College, Philadelphia, came to Lord's for exhibition in 2010.

**Major Wharton's Tour of South Africa, 1888–9**
**Photographed by G.F. Fearneyhough**
**Donated to MCC by Miss E.H. Wharton, 1967**
The side suffered unexpected defeats early in the tour, the result – according to one of the players' accounts – of over-generous hospitality. The players of both sides here enjoy a picnic during their time away from the playing field.

Both an MCC and an Australian team were tempted to Hollywood during that period, and for similar reasons teams touring England traditionally opened their accounts in the heartland of Sussex cricket at the Duke of Norfolk's Ground at Arundel, or in earlier days at Sheffield Park. The ground there was recently reincarnated by the Armadillos Club in partnership with the National Trust. It was the toast of the town in the late nineteenth century, with arguably the most picturesque pavilions of any ground and views out over gardens modelled by both Capability Brown and Humphry Repton. Teams such as the Parsees, the first tourists from India, were famously photographed in front of its wrought-iron balconies and floral displays. It is clear that no expense was spared. Sheffield had just spent £16,000 on the 1891–2 tour to Australia, incurring a £2,000 loss, but went further, like Donald Currie, donating money to the Australian Cricket Council to realise the Sheffield Shield, the prize for the winners of the Australian first-class competition. The shield was recently restored and appeared at the "Old England/Australia" match (p.116) at Sheffield Park in 2009 en route to exhibition at Lord's.

The importance of such patrons in the staging of cricket was mirrored at Lord's, where they played an essential role in the Ground's rise to prominence. Thomas Lord, the founder, was not so intent on leaving his name to posterity that he was beyond threatening to sell off a significant portion of the Ground to development. In this case, William Ward's status as a Bank of England director was more important than his reputation as one of the greatest players of his day: he stepped in to write the cheque. In the Museum his account book sits symbolically alongside the ball of his 1820 innings of 278 – a record first-class score broken only by a W.G. Grace triple-century. Ward in turn sold the lease to James Dark,

**Lord's staff outing, 1920s**
**Loaned to MCC by the**
**Portman Family**
George Portman organised an annual outing for his catering staff which more often than not involved a Thames boat trip from Marlow, lunch and a cricket match.

who, in a loyal gesture, offered MCC first option when he retired after 40 years at Lord's.

Four years earlier the Club had ignored the chance to purchase the freehold from the Eyre estate, despite Dark's urging. In 1866, on the counsel of the President and newly appointed Secretary, it reconsidered and at last became the owner of its premises outright. Money was forwarded at a preferential rate of interest at this crucial juncture by William Nicholson (p.112). His largesse continued to flow with a loan to fund the building of the Lord's Hotel, and then more importantly the construction of the new Pavilion in 1889–90.

Nicholson was a wealthy director of the J. & W. Nicholson Distillery Company, founded in 1730s in Clerkenwell during the gin craze, and established tidal mills – the largest in the world – on the River Lea in Newham. With perfect symmetry both the Pavilion, a product of his proceeds, and the Mill, which was responsible for his wealth, are now listed by English Heritage as buildings of outstanding architectural interest.

Though these examples of financial patronage were immensely significant, they were matched in human terms by the dynasties of staff during decades of

**I Zingari at Lord's, 1864**
**Photographer unknown**
Standing on the balcony is Francis (Frank) Dark, scion of the Dark family. James was the proprietor of Lord's from 1835; his brothers Ben and Robert made bats and balls and organised the gate on big match days. Ben's daughter Matilda took over the business on his death and passed it on to Frank. They surrendered the tenancy in the year of this photograph.

employment at Lord's. The founder's name predominates, of course, but for much of the nineteenth century the Ground was known as Dark's. James Henry Dark perhaps did more for Lord's than any other man but has never been honoured in any of the Club's subsequent celebrations; born in Edgware Road and resident at Lord's for the majority of his life, his grave lies unrestored less than three miles away in the cemetery in Kensal Green.

He married into a hotel proprietor's family (Lathom) and, using his wife's dowry to purchase the leasehold of the Ground from William Ward, exploited the experience of his new relations to run the Tavern until the 1840s. His own family quickly settled; one brother, Ben, started a bat-making business behind the tennis court in a workshop adjoining the stables. His stacks of seasoning willow blocks were a familiar feature of the south-east corner of Lord's. James's other brother Robert took over the upper floor of the tennis court above the newly built billiards room to make "leg-guards" and balls. He and James, along with their relative John, who owned a profitable local dustman's business and whose relatives were the first tenants of the Lord's Hotel, all lived along the St John's Wood Road on the south side of the Ground. When James died unexpectedly, his widow Matilda took up the reins. Of the next generation, Francis (Frank), the wicketkeeper and batsman of the family, "purchased James' interest" in Lord's as well as the bat business from Matilda, while Sydney Dark, nephew of James, worked as assistant secretary and clerk to MCC from 1862 to 1871.

Stephen (known as Steevey) Slatter had lodged with James Dark long before Dark took up the tenancy at Lord's. He arrived with him and continued to work at the Ground for over 40 years, dying in the very same year as his employer. William Slatter, his son, wrote a colourful memoir while still in post as Clerk of Works in 1914. He recorded his impressions of over 50 years' service since he first started work aged ten in 1861. As with the Darks, so with the Slatters: William's brother worked at Lord's for 40 years, and his own son Steve for eighteen years before his untimely death. His maternal grandmother and paternal aunt died as pensioners of MCC, char and cleaning women respectively. His mother, still alive in 1914 aged 89, was the laundress, and his sister, born at Lord's, was in charge of Mound Stand ladies' room.

Dick Gaby started work at Lord's in Slatter's time, aged fifteen in 1875; among other things, he was the scoreboard operator and marker for lawn tennis courts on non-match days. He retired in 1938 at the age of 78, after 63 years' service. His son, Dick Junior, was a relatively late starter taking his first job at 21 as telegraph boy, ringing through bets to bookmakers. He stayed on until 1973, almost 100 years after his father had first arrived.

**Irish Cricketers, Western Australia, 1896**
**Photographer unknown**
Inscribed on reverse: "The man with the gun is the Umpire as it is necessary for all umpires to carry a gun in Western Australia." This is thought to be a team of miners, possibly from Kalgoorlie.

During much of their time George Portman ran the catering business. Promoted in 1902 when the Committee were at their wits' end, he turned the business around, living above the hotel with his wife Lydia, who ran the café that opened onto the St John's Wood Road, and his daughter who, with her friends, spent many happy summers churning butter and ice in great buckets for Lord's famous home-made ice-cream. Much to his chagrin, his failing health persuaded the Club to replace him after 48 years' service.

Before Dick Gaby Junior retired, it was the turn of a fourth family to take up the tradition. By the mid-1970s, three generations of Hawkes had started work around the Ground and their presence on the staff remains to this very day. With more people employed at Lord's than ever before one might expect that such traditions would be set to continue. However, the transitory nature of the contemporary job market and harsh economic times threaten even the sanctuary of MCC.

# Dust to Dust

Ivo Bligh, captain of the England XI, addressed his hosts at a farewell dinner at the Melbourne Cricket Ground at the end of the three-match series against the Australian XI: "This amusement about 'The Ashes' has served us well," he said, "but perhaps it is time to bury the joke in a quiet corner of the MCG where it may be forgotten."

**Ashes celebration at The Oval, 2009 Photographed by Tom Shaw, Getty Images**
It has become customary for a replica Ashes Urn to be used during victory celebrations, though the Waterford Crystal Urn is the official trophy for the series.

**I've washed that ugly old egg cup thing …**
**Watercolour and pencil cartoon by Stan McMurtry (2005)**
The caption continues: "It was full of ashes." McMurtry (Mac) has been the cartoonist for the *Daily Mail* for over 30 years and was created MBE in 2003.

Despite Bligh's request, the ladies responsible for the initial gift of the Ashes Urn were not for turning, and by the time he left Australia a victory verse, snipped from a newspaper, had been glued to the Urn, which he now carried in a velvet bag embroidered with his initials and dated 1883.

Its original presentation had taken place at the home of Lord and Lady Clarke, Rupertswood, just outside Melbourne on Christmas Eve 1882. The amateurs of the English side were guests of the Clarkes and had played their part (batting and sitting in the shade mostly) against the estate team; they finished victorious and Lady Clarke, in her resourcefulness, unearthed their prize, the tiny ceramic urn. She even directed one of her staff – whose family bear

testament to the story – to burn a bail to realise some actual ashes; the embodiment of the joke played out among the press since Australia's momentous first win on English soil that August.

The diminutive treasure returned to England and stood sentinel on Bligh's mantelpiece until such time as it was dusted off by a clumsy maid. Such was the (seemingly apocryphal) story that accompanied its donation to Lord's in 1927. For 75 years it sat unchecked, but X-rays in 2002 (taken for insurance purposes) revealed the presence of a slender bolt holding the Urn together, confirming the tale. Why the thoughtful restoration? Not just a prize, it was a love token too, a symbol of the captain's first encounter with his future wife at Rupertswood.

**William Nicholson** by
**Frank Holl, RA (1879)
Loaned by Tim Walker, Esq.,
2011**
William Nicholson had a
long amateur career after
he attended Harrow and
Cambridge. However, he is
better known for the significant
part he played off the field in
MCC history. It was his money
that finally enabled the Club

to purchase the freehold of
the Ground in 1864, then to
build the Tavern and Hotel and
finally the Pavilion in 1889–90.
By family tradition, MCC
acknowledged this by changing
its Club colours, although there
is no mention in its archive
papers. The red and yellow
Nicholson Gin labels still remain
the likeliest of templates and
the one-time nickname of "Gin

Palace" was not unjustified.
His portrait here hangs at the
north entrance to the Pavilion.
The artist, who lived and
died close to Lord's in North
London, was well respected and
completed numerous portraits
for the Royal Family, aristocracy
and leading members of
government.

**K.S. Ranjitsinhji's pocket watch and cigarette case, 1756 and 1912**
Bequeathed by E. Rockley Wilson, 1957; purchased at auction, 2003
Ball from Fry and Ranji's "big partnership", loaned by Ken Medlock, Esq., 2007

K.S. Ranjitsinhji, the Maharajah Jam Sahib of Nawanagar, was one of the great figures of cricket's Golden Age. His skill on the field is undoubted and this was matched by his notoriety as the self-styled "Prince" Ranji. Constantly dogged by a string of creditors, he was nevertheless a generous host in later years, entertaining at Ballynahinch Castle in Connemara and Shillinglee Park in Sussex. He was famously photographed with the great W.G. Grace and of course C.B. Fry with whom he shared a great many batting partnerships (the one commemorated on this ball is still to be identified). The pocket watch at one time belonged to the great cricketer David Harris, then to Lord Harris, and it was subsequently owned by Ranji before being gifted to MCC.

Sheet music, late nineteenth and early twentieth centuries
Variously donated to MCC by Wing Cdr Featherstone, Mr J. Rowland, Mr P. Robinson, Oxford University Press et al, 1957–72

"Today many of these songs written for smoking concerts and Club dinners seem quaint, trite, jingoistic and musically banal and make strange bedfellows with some of the flip offerings of recent years," writes David Rayvern Allen in *A Song for Cricket*. "Yet in each case there is an accurate reflection of the social attitudes, humour and standards prevalent at the time, and if the *lingua franca* has changed, it was just as significant to the people of its age. The cricket song tells its own history, which deserves to be preserved."

**The BBC National Radio Award presented to Brian Johnston, 1988**
**Various Gramophone Records, 1920s–1960s**
**Variously loaned and donated to MCC, from 1950s**

Brian Johnston, the stalwart of *Test Match Special* from 1970 to 1993 and mentor to Christopher Martin-Jenkins (see pp.162–3), was described as "the voice of summer". He was enormously popular and is remembered at Lord's in the creation of the Museum's film theatre, funded by the generosity of John Paul Getty. Musical celebrations of cricket are no more joyful than in the recorded songs of calypsonians such as Lord Kitchener, Egbert Moore, David Rudder and Cy Grant. Though MCC has collected only a few examples there are literally hundreds, from their emergence at the end of the nineteenth century through the great years of West Indian cricket to the present day.

**Menu from the dinner to the South Africans held at Sheffield Park, 1894 Bequeathed to MCC by E. Rockley Wilson, 1957**

Lord Sheffield, who was instrumental in the creation of the Australian domestic trophy, was the illustrious host of cricket matches at his home in Sussex. Matches are thought to date from the 1850s but the 3rd Earl's side played between 1881 and 1896. The picturesque ground with ornate pavilions was a backdrop for the famous touring sides of the day, watched by crowds – always admitted for free – of up to 25,000. After his death the ground was not kept up but in 2009, with the agreement of the National Trust and help of Sussex CCC, the Armadillos Cricket Club resurrected it for an inaugural match between vintage England and Australian sides.

**Ceramics by Doulton, New Hall, Sandland and Staffordshire**
**Variously acquired by MCC, 1950–2010**

This selection of jugs and mugs is decorated with players from the seventeenth to twentieth centuries, from Fuller Pilch to W.G. Grace, Hobbs and Sutcliffe to Hedley Verity. They stand testament not only to the wonderful social traditions of cricket reaching back to the times of Richard Nyren at The Bat and Ball Inn, but also to the analogous rise of the great English ceramic industry of the late eighteenth and nineteenth centuries. Josiah Wedgwood was into his stride and had hired John Flaxman, protégé of Thomas Hope (see p.222), as MCC was starting to make its mark. Doulton, founded in 1815 in Lambeth, likewise went from strength to strength in the Victorian era, culminating in a Royal Warrant in 1901. All the firms made the most of celebrity figures such as Fuller Pilch and W.G. Grace, who appears in countless guises on innumerable different pots.

**William Davies by Thomas Henwood (1842)**
**Acquired by MCC, after 1914 and before 1939**

This portrait of the Sussex and Lewes Club's scorer is one of the most endearing images in the collection. Clearly a significant figure on the Sussex scene, he is pictured at his task with Lewes Castle in the background. The tools of his trade include a measuring tape as well as the playing equipment, lending him an authority which is today divided between umpire, scorer and groundsman. Current scorers, installed in their new box at Lord's, directly beneath Father Time, now score the whole game digitally, ending the tradition of pen and paper that stretches back to the eighteenth century.

**MCC 50th anniversary rummer by Royal Brierley Crystal, 1837**
**Donated by H.J. Stevenson, 1921**

The scene depicts Lord's during the jubilee match between North and South; William Lillywhite (of the Piccadilly sports store dynasty) took fourteen wickets. "There was then the public house, a long low building on the south side, separated from the ground by a row of clipped lime trees and a few green benches on which thirsty spectators smoked long pipes and enjoyed drinks. Round the ground there were more of these small benches without backs, and a pot-boy walked round with a supply of beer, a porter for the public who had no other means of refreshing themselves." The post-match banquet "was served up in Mr Dark's usual excellent style and consisted of every delicacy of the season".

**Tsunami Match Photo Collage by David Buckland Commissioned by MCC, 2005**

In the wake of the terrible destruction wreaked by the Indonesian tidal wave on Boxing Day 2004, a series of charity cricket matches were played culminating in that at Lord's. Players flew in from all around the world, Chris Gayle literally arriving from the airport in time to change and walk straight out to play. The match raised over £650,000, which was used to help rebuild Galle cricket ground in Sri Lanka and create the MCC Centre of Excellence in Seenigama, providing extra funding for the Foundation for Goodness charity led by Kushil Gunasekera and supported by Muttiah Muralidaran and Kumar Sangakkara.

TSUNAMI RELIEF MATCH

Sachin Tendulkar    Chris Cairns     VVS Laxman    Makhaya Ntini
Chris Gayle                 Mike Gatting (Coach, MCC)
                                         Shane Warne

C.C. v **INTERNATIONAL XI**  LORD'S  Tuesday, 14th June 2005

Darrell Hair [Umpire]  John Holder [Umpire]  Shoaib Akhtar  Shaun Pollock  Anil Kumble  Kumar Sangakkara
Jacques Kallis  Stephen Fleming [Captain, MCC]  Rodney Marsh [Coach, Int.XI]  Rahul Dravid  Sourav Ganguly  Andy Flower
ath Jayasuriya  Mohammad Sami  Shivnarine Chanderpaul  Virender Sehwag
Brian Lara [Captain, International XI]  Chaminda Vaas  Graeme Smith  Portrait by Buckland 2005

W. WASHINGTON
1934

The Cricket Bat Maker.                                    Wᵐ Washington

**The Cricket Bat Maker** by
**William Washington (1934)**
**Acquired by MCC from Parker**
**Galleries, 1949**

In the seventeenth century
cricket bats were made by
general woodworkers, but soon
demand resulted in specialist
firms who began to stamp
their marks on the handles
or feet. This beautiful copper
engraving, an artist's proof, is
from a series on the subject of
craftsmanship. The batmaker
is thought to be Ben Warsop,
whose family firm was founded
in 1870, had a factory on Park
Road in St John's Wood, and
still produces handcrafted
bats in Essex. It appears as an
illustration in Hugh Barty-King's
*Quilt Winders and Podshavers*,
published in 1979 but still the
most authoritative work on
the subject.

**Leg Theory**, a cartoon
by "Spurll"
**Acquired by MCC,**
**date unknown**

A short note is appended
to this framed drawing that
reads: "Notice to Umpires:
The Committee having taken
a serious view of the physical
danger involved by the use of
Leg Theory bowling, hereby
instruct that before the
commencement of any Test
Match Australian or otherwise
that the offending stump be
withdrawn for the duration of
the War (crossed out) Match.
Signed MCC."

**Gradidge bat used by
Bert Oldfield in the "Bodyline"
Series, 1932
Donated to MCC by
Mrs W.A. Oldfield, 1976**

From 1924 to 1937 Bert
Oldfield missed only one
Test Match, the fourth of the
infamous Bodyline series.
During the previous game in
Adelaide he had top-edged a
ball from Harold Larwood and
fractured his skull. He was
carried unconscious from the
ground, but still took his place
in the line-up for the final match
of the series. He never blamed
Larwood for the incident and
when Larwood emigrated to
Australia late in life the two
became firm friends.

**A Silver Cigarette Box inscribed to Douglas Jardine by members of the 1932–3 English Touring team to Australia**

**Donated to MCC by Association of Cricket Umpires and Scorers, 2009**

This tour has been discussed more than any other in the history of cricket. Douglas Jardine, England's victorious captain, was shunned by the crowds, by the opposition, by MCC and by the team manager. It was not that he had employed unusual or at least unfamiliar tactics, it was just that he and his team mates had executed them far more effectively than anyone had before. Don Bradman, the ostensible target of aggressive short-pitched bowling, never spoke of either Jardine or "Bodyline" and MCC declined to consider the request by Jardine's family to scatter his ashes at Lord's.

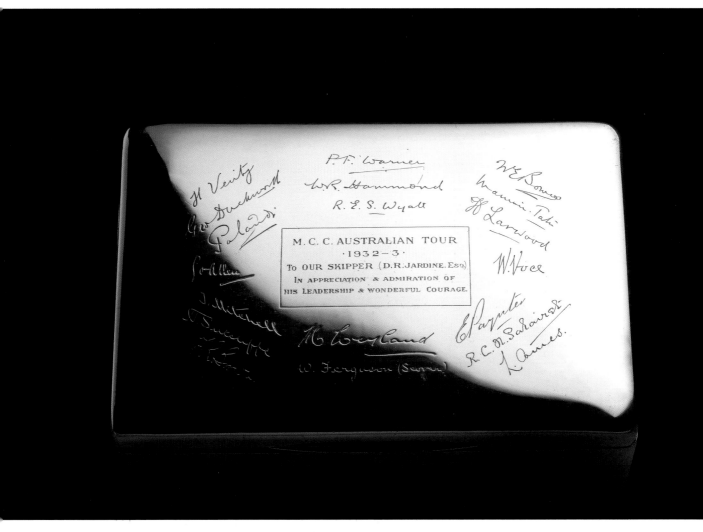

# Spirit of Cricket

The portraits of Donald Bradman and Douglas Jardine have always provoked comment. Ted Dexter suggested they never be hung together – his response to Jardine betraying the values of "fair play". Some in turn demanded they never be apart, symbolising the intense competition that sport engenders. The Ashes series of 2005 exemplified how both these attitudes blend into the "spirit" of cricket: Lee and Flintoff's cameraderie, made more affecting by their burning desire to win.

**Brett Lee's match ball, 2009**
**Photographed by**
**Clare Skinner, loaned to**
**MCC, 2009–12**
Brett Lee's five-wicket haul is not celebrated on the honours boards as it was achieved in a One-Day International.

**Glenn McGrath in the
MCC Museum, 2005
Photographed by
Anthony Devlin**
McGrath celebrates his 500th
Test wicket alongside the
Ashes Urn (see also p.269).

## A Landmark
Glenn McGrath

Midway through my career I set a goal of taking 500 Test wickets. I felt if I could get there I would have achieved what I wanted to in Test cricket.

Before the 2005 Ashes Series, we toured New Zealand. I finished that series on 499 wickets, which set the stage for a potential 500th wicket at Lord's against England. Ricky Ponting joked at the time I was trying my best not to get the last wicket in Auckland – not true!

Our turn to bowl came just before tea on that first day. First ball back after tea, from the Pavilion End, I came in off my long run. With my natural swing, hitting the wicket and moving away down the slope from the left-hander, the ball straightened and went across Marcus Trescothick; seeing Justin Langer take the catch was something I will always remember.

I look back on that day with great joy. My parents and various other family members were in the crowd. We won the Test and I was fortunate enough to go on to take nine wickets in the match. I had achieved my goal at the home of cricket, against England in an Ashes Series. Amazing.

Each time I've been back to Lord's I make a point of walking out onto the pitch, down the halls and through the players' rooms, soaking in all of the history and tradition. It always sends tingles down my spine. Seeing my name on the wall alongside some of the legends of world cricket is humbling and something I am enormously proud of. Three matches, three wins against England and three Man of the Match awards!

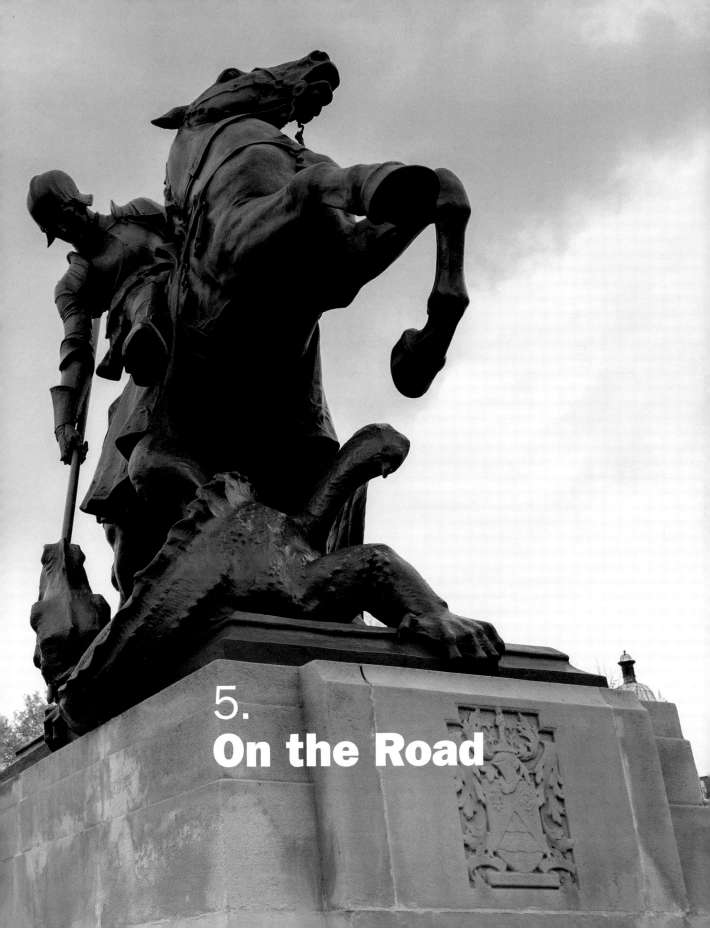

# 5.
# On the Road

At long last, at least as far as the Australian public and Cricket Australia were concerned, the Ashes Urn arrived in Australia in 2006. It was not destined to stay, as some of the players had demanded, and indeed as some leading commentators – notably Matthew Engel, the editor of *Wisden* – had also suggested. The Urn was on tour, not as the trophy for that year's Ashes series (the first since the monumental 2005 contest), but to explain exactly why it was *not* the trophy and in so doing to lay bare its origins.

A whistle-stop tour of the cities hosting Test Matches had been arranged as part of a touring Ashes exhibition. Given the appointment of the Tasmanian Keith Bradshaw as Secretary of MCC that autumn, it was no surprise that Hobart was added as a final stop on the itinerary for the Urn after the exhibition's departure. All professional precautions had been taken, not least an X-ray for the insurers back in 2002, which had not only proved the Urn was fractured but as a consequence had delayed its departure by a four-year Ashes cycle.

It was a far cry from its last trip to Sydney in 1988, when it had travelled to take part in the bicentennial celebrations of the European settlement of Australia. It had at that time, according to legend, travelled in the handbag of the Secretary's wife on the royal flight; metaphorically very apt, given its possible origin as a scent bottle, but rather unconventional to say the least. Similarly its return from the *Sporting Glory* exhibition at the Victoria and Albert Museum in 1992–3 had been a little unorthodox, cradled by the Curator in the passenger seat of the Club van.

Previous pages: *St George and the Dragon* by C.L. Hartwell, RA, outside St John's Wood Church. Cast by Morris Singer (1936–7). Photographed by Graham Morris.The adjacent Wellington Road roundabout used to be known as "Coffin Corner" in the early days of Lord's Ground. The statue mirrors the image that appeared on the pocket of MCC touring blazers from 1903 until 1997.

**Cricket in St Kitts, 1895**
**Donated to MCC by**
**Teddington CC, 1957**

This is a scene from one of the thirteen matches played by the first English touring XI to the West Indies in 1894–5. The players were all amateurs, and of them only two had played any first-class cricket in recent years. The scorebook is also in the archive at Lord's.

In hindsight its unorthodox travels echo the tales of the first touring cricket teams, who suffered no small discomforts in reaching their destinations, but once there received on the whole enthusiastic if not rapturous receptions. Ivo Bligh's XI of 1882 took four months to tour Australia and endured a further fourteen weeks' passage on board the steamship *Peshawur*. Their ship out of Colombo actually collided with another vessel, injuring one of their players, and causing a delay of many days. When finally they arrived, they were given a boisterous welcome at 2am and no excuse was brooked to play their opening fixture that afternoon at 2pm. This tour followed Australia's great triumph in England, the match that sparked the whole Ashes story. As such there was a stronger than usual rivalry, even though Murdoch's team – the famous victors in the Oval match of 1882 – were not to reach Australia until after Bligh's was well into its stride. As in the case of so many subsequent tours, particularly those involving Lord Hawke,

the main aim was to proselytise and to expand the cricket-playing boundaries around the globe.

Hawke was an MCC President and Treasurer during the First World War and into the 1930s, but prior to this he was one of the most prolific tourists of the age. He enrolled on nine tours altogether during his playing career between 1887 and 1912. His maiden tour, which was to Australia (p.142), was curtailed shortly after he arrived by the death of his father, but he subsequently travelled twice to India and Ceylon, South Africa and North America and visited the West Indies and Argentina. Many of the matches he played were not first-class and the quality of his sides was often thought useful rather than outstanding.

He also held strong convictions with regard to "England" tours as the twentieth century dawned, refusing to allow Yorkshire players to be released for them, arguing that Yorkshire, the county of which he was President, should retain but compensate them. J.M. Kilburn wrote that he believed strongly in sponsorship of England tours and home Tests and thought that MCC should take on this responsibility. On MCC's acceptance of this, Hawke happily granted leave to Yorkshire players, content in the knowledge that just as much consideration would be shown to them by MCC as by Yorkshire.

The assumption of responsibility for England tours by MCC resulted in the 1903 tour to Australia, led by Pelham Warner (see pp.214–15). His selection as captain, given the extra emphasis on it being a representative national side, proved quite controversial and there was perhaps more discussion than usual of the make-up of the team. What was more fascinating from a historical perspective was the re-emergence of the word "Ashes" in association with a cricket series. Warner dedicated his travelogue "to the Members of MCC as whose representatives we fought our battles on Australian wickets and for whose credit we are proud to have brought home the ashes of victory". He noted the attention given by the newspapers to the regaining of "the Ashes", and to the cartoon in the pages of *Punch* in which the kangaroo gave back the Ashes to the lion.

This set the tone of the next 60 to 70 years as tour programme after tour programme, cartoonist after cartoonist, player after player imagined different Ashes trophies and wrote, drew, and even created and gifted their own versions. Owing to MCC's management of the tours, the archive at Lord's contains a great wealth of information including scorebooks, tour reports and souvenirs, and, in association with the Melbourne Club's records of Australian tours, presents a wonderful and reciprocal social history of their times.

Given the amount of time spent travelling, the off-field activities of the players were as much a part of a tour as the on-field exploits, and particularly in those instances where the aim of the tour was to "spread the word". Moreover, it was an age when social niceties were of paramount importance. Ceylon proved a popular staging post en route to the Antipodes and soon it was almost as popular with some of the tourists as Australia. No doubt the practical role it played was responsible for the deep roots that cricket put down.

Anthony Meredith in *Summers in Winter* relates that "few of the players spent seven months of celibacy with much resolution". One imagines their resolution was particularly tested in 1946 when the team travelled on the *Stirling Castle*, which was transporting 600 war brides to Australia.

Stephen Fay, writing for the MCC magazine, goes on: "One, asked how he spent his time on-board ship in 1936, replied, 'Chasing bints mostly'. In those days it was a case of 'no name, no pack drill' amongst the cricket writers but [Neville] Cardus might have let his hair down a bit when he reported: '[George] Duckworth danced each evening with a nice understanding of what, socially, he was doing'." Given the close proximity of team and reporters, it is a surprise to find none of this in the newspapers or cable and telegrams, but hints do surface

**MCC Tour of India Scrapbook, 1926–7**
**Donated to MCC by the Madras CC, 1926–7**
This page illustrates both the players and spectators from the match in Madras. Viscount Goschen, Governor of Madras at the time and future acting Viceroy (1929–31), is pictured at top right.

occasionally in players' private correspondence and scrapbooks. Gubby Allen left his scrapbooks on the "Bodyline" tour of 1932–3 to MCC, but this was a far more controversial trip, and while the outward journey was recorded in light-hearted fashion – with cartoons by Arthur Mailey among others – his scrapbooks remain conservative compared to others.

The guidelines issued to players by MCC to prepare them for the touring life sometimes prove unintentionally amusing. *Cricket in Hot Climates* (1954) gives the following doctor's advice for sunburn: "In some personal experiments connected with similar burns from atomic bombs, I found that anti-histamine creams …

**'I ain't heard nothing about a cricket match …'
by Giles (1967)
Donated and inscribed to
MCC by the artist**
The Yorkshire team at the time faced allegations of persistent time-wasting in order to draw out games to prevent defeat.

'I ain't heard nothing about a cricket match between Yorkshire and the Vietcong, have you Hank?'

To The Marylebone C.C.,
from Giles.
'67

reduced the 'ache'." For over-indulgence he advises: "After liberal hospitality, try to prevent a hangover by drinking a pint of fruit juice or water with a salt tablet. If you have a hangover, take 2 Alka Seltzers, drink a lot of water, try to take some breakfast, lie down for half an hour … don't smoke yet."

Nevertheless, the jewels of the scrapbook archive relate to tours in the UK, primarily by the wandering clubs. After Felix's record of the All-England XI (p.138), those of I Zingari are the foremost of these, crammed with photographs, sketches, rhymes, jokes, scraps and just about every form of wordplay imaginable. Divided into cricket seasons and mingled with much theatrical material, they rather reflect the Canterbury Cricket Festival, in which several of the club members were involved as the Old Stagers, by repute the oldest amateur dramatic society in the world. They were cricketers first and actors second, who "devoted themselves indefatigably to the game [of cricket] during the day, and found comparatively little time for rehearsals. Scenes were rehearsed in corners of the cricket field or in the dressing tent, at any odd moments that were available. Nothing but the indefatigable energy of youth, combined with an intense love for theatricals, could have kept the ball a-rolling when once started."

They prove rich sources for the activities not only of Sir Spencer Ponsonby-Fane but also the then Secretary of MCC, R.A. Fitzgerald. In the 1870s Fitzgerald stood up to William Gladstone when the government expressed displeasure at the prospect of a touring side heading to North America, and it seems that threat of political intervention has never been permanently scotched since. Perhaps the most obvious examples were the controversy over the 1970 South African tour (p.143), which resulted in threats against the Lord's square, and of course the subsequent rebel tours to South Africa.

After 1965, the sea voyages were no more and the joy of travel seems to have metaphorically steamed off over the horizon. There is after all a limit to the excitement and variety provided on an aeroplane, unless you are David Boon. In the words of Stephen Fay again, "the travelling … has become an exhausting, comfortless chore". I can't imagine there is much scrapbooking now, and England no longer even takes a scorer with the team. Tours are increasingly at the mercy of major tournaments such as the ICC World Cups, not to mention the Indian Premier League (IPL), and at the time of writing England will face Australia in ten Test Matches and countless One-Day Internationals, not to mention Twenty20 matches, in the next nine months. Not so much cultural exchange as naked commercialism. The tour is dead, long live the tour!

# River Snake … Thames

The first Australian cricket team to tour England was an Australian Aboriginal XI who played at Lord's in 1868. The scorecard shown here advertises the lunchtime entertainment provided by the tourists in a match they played at Blackheath, London; the Boammer opposite was used by Dick-a-Dick when he was "dodging cricket balls". The poem by the Aboriginal poet Rikki Shields is taken from the MCC poetry anthology *A Breathless Hush* and was performed at the book launch in the Long Room in 2004.

PRICE 3 PENCE.

# CORRECT SCORE.

At BLACKHEATH.  AUSTRALIAN ELEVEN v. BLACKHEATH

Monday, & Tuesday, September 21, & 22, 1868.

| BLACKHEATH | First Innings | | Second Inning | |
|---|---|---|---|---|
| P. M. Thornton, Esq | c Twopenny, b Lawrence | 0 | c Lawrence, b Red Cap | 10 |
| E. Wade, Esq | b Mullagh | 11 | b Mullagh | 1 |
| W. Coppinger | c Peter, b Mullagh | 23 | run out | 19 |
| E. T. Coppinger, Esq | c Twopenny b Cuzens | 16 | c Red Cap | 4 |
| J. C. Gregory, Esq | b Lawrence | 18 | c Mullagh, b Red Cap | 7 |
| W. L. Pierce, Esq | c Cuzens, b Mullagh | 0 | b Cuzens | 0 |
| T. A. Raynes, Esq | b Cuzens | 31 | b Mullagh | 16 |
| J. S. Miller, Esq | b Cuzens | 0 | b Red Cap | 3 |
| R. De Zoete, Esq | c Red Cap, b Lawrence | 4 | b Cuzens | 4 |
| F. Russell, Esq | b Lawrence | 3 | not out | 0 |
| T. Scard, Esq | not out | 1 | c Lawrence, b Cuzens | 2 |

b 8  l-b 5  w 1  n-b , 14    b 9 , l-b , w , n-b , 9

Total 121        Total 75

| AUSTRALIAN | First Innings | | Second Innings | |
|---|---|---|---|---|
| Cuzens (white) | c Gregory, b Wade | 0 | b Russell | 10 |
| Mullagh (dark blue) | c Gregory, b W Coppinger | 13 | st E Copingr b W Copgr | 36 |
| Tiger (pink) | b Wade | 7 | st E T Coppinger b W Copgr | 8 |
| Bullocky (moroon) | l b w. b Russell | 15 | st E T Coppinger b Wade | 4 |
| Twopenny (light blue) | b Wade | 10 | b Russell | 6 |
| C. Lawrence, Captain | c Miller, b Wade | 6 | b Raynes | 25 |
| Red Cap (black) | not out | 3 | c Pierce, b Wade | 9 |
| Peter (green) | b Russell | 0 | b Russell | 3 |
| Charley (brown) | b Wade | 0 | st E Copinger b W Copgr | 22 |
| Mosquito (majento) | b Wade | 0 | not out | 2 |
| Dick-a-Dick (yellow) | c an b b Wade | 0 | b Wade | 5 |

b 8  l-b 2 , w 3  n-b , 13    b 3 l-b , w 4 , n-b 1 8

Umpires  Shepherd & R. Irwin    Total 67        Total 116

## AUSTRALIAN SPORTS

Throwing Spears and Boomerangs in Native Costume

Lawrences's Feat with Bat and Ball

Dick-a-Dick Dodging Cricket Ball

AUSTRALIAN ABORIGINES v. THE GENTLEMEN of MIDDLESEX

WEDNESDAY & THURSDAY SEPTEMBER, 23, & 24, AT THE

## MIDDLESEX COUNTY CRICKET GROUND.

CALEDONIAN ROAD ISLINGTON.

Scorecard from the Aboriginal tour of England, 1868. Acquired by MCC, date unknown.

### *The Last Over* by Rikki Shields

In memory of King Cole, Aboriginal Cricketer who died on 24th June 1868

Your Aboriginal dreamtime home. Wish you peace. Nyuntu Anangu
    Tjukapa Wiltja Nga Palya Nga.

Legend of the Southern Cross Stars that light the night-sky over Australia.
Seven Aboriginal Women fetch the wood at sundown. Then they fly into the
    sky
and make seven campfires, while they wait eternally for the lost warriors to
    return home.

1866 was a Stormy night as the women watched the wooden ship sailing
from Botany Bay, inside the ship were twelve gallant warriors
They went as Ambassadors in Games and Humanity, To play this strange
    sport...... Cricket.
Behind their land was ravaged and claimed in the name of fair play

Loyoranna the Wind, blew the ship, across mountainous Seas
Then finally to the River Snake... Thames.

London Town where Clay People dwell, Who rule by class, Stone hearts,
Darkness, No Fire in the Sky.

The Cricket warriors knew the dangers if they failed on this Mission
Wondrous people did they meet, the old, Young, but not Politicians.

then tragedy struck off spinner bowler, Sugar, Died where-abouts unknown.
Chief King Cole passed away in white-fella death house at St Guy's
No Sacred Ceremony, No Weeping Women, to help their bones and spirit
    return
to their beginning time

Did the evil Clayface Doctor swap Kings bones for their own?
Does he sit in a Shoe Box or glass jar in Royal College of Surgeons
in central London Town... We'll never know.

Yet the seven Aboriginal Women night fire shines brightly
The Women still Weeping, still hoping.

There is humanity in this hostile jungle city of London
The People of Tower Hamlets, Erected a stone for the Journey
And memory of Our Dusky Warrior of Cricket
Ambassador King Cole...

The names of other members in team were: SUGAR, NEDDY, JELLICO,
    COUSINS,
MULLAGH, BULLOCKY, TARPOT, SUNDOWN, OFFICER, PETER and
    CAPTAIN.

**Boammer, 1860s (detail).**
The whole club is shown on
p.62.

***All-England Lost by Night
on Holbeach Marsh* by
"Felix" (1851–2)**
**From the sketchbook donated
to MCC by Colonel N. King,
1944**
One of the first "travelogues"
of a team was kept by Nicholas
Wanostrocht, known as "Felix",
an accomplished artist as
well as one of the "Eleven of
All-England". He kept a journal
which he wrote and illustrated
as the team toured the British

Isles playing to packed houses.
It was organised by William
Clarke, one-time Ground bowler
at Lord's and employee of
MCC. Dissatisfied with his
wage, in 1845 he formed the
All-England XI, showcasing the
best players of the day and
making a significant amount of
money. A somewhat dictatorial
figure, he drove the players
so hard that eventually a rival
team, the United England XI,
was formed.

**All-England at Lord's,
5th June 1865
Donated to MCC by
Mrs E. Davies, 1968**

In 1861 the SS *Great Britain*
carried the first ever England
side to tour Australia, made
up of players from the rival
All-England and United England
teams. Large numbers of
live animals were carried for
food, rendering the ship to all
intents and purposes a floating
barnyard for the 2½-month
voyage. The tourists arrived
back in England almost seven
months after they set out. In
1865 the two all-star sides
were still touring around
England and they met at Lord's.
The All-England XI that emerged
victorious was led by George
Parr (standing fourth from left),
a veteran of overseas tours,
having captained the 1859
tour to the USA (see pp.39,
191) and the 1864 team to
Australia.

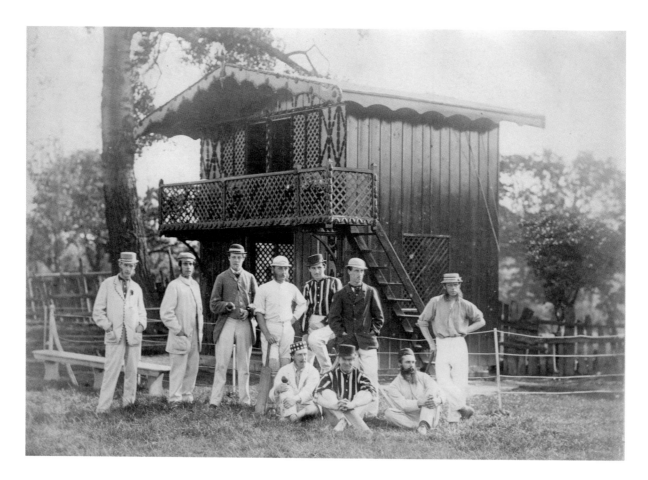

**Incogniti CC, Staffordshire, 1865**
**Acquired by MCC, date unknown**

The Incogniti are one of the oldest of the wandering clubs, founded in 1861, when they played their first game at Lord's. Although they initially made Tufnell Park their home, it was soon abandoned and they have remained truly nomadic, playing games all over the world through 150 seasons. The tradition of the wandering or "homeless" club is a particular feature of English cricket and derives from the late nineteenth century, after the founding in 1845 of I Zingari – "The Gypsies". It has generated literally hundreds of subsequent "troupes" that range from the archetypal genres of authors or actors to those such as the infamous Captain Scott XI, named after the personification of British heroic failure.

An Original English Lady Cricketers' costume worn by "Molly Beckenham", 1890 Donated to MCC by Miss Netta Rheinberg, Women's Cricket Association, 1957

The Original English Lady Cricketers were formed in 1890 and backed by James Lillywhite's *Cricketers Annual*. Splitting into two teams – the Reds and Blues – the women all played under pseudonyms, had chaperones as well as a manager, and were paid sixpence a day expenses. They played exhibition matches around the country, and their first match in Liverpool attracted over 15,000 spectators. Their success continued until their manager absconded with the profits.

**The prayer book of the Hon. M.B. Hawke, 1887**
**Yorkshire cufflinks belonging to Lord Hawke**
**Loaned by C. Ridley Esq., 2008**

Martin Bladen, the Hon. M.B. Hawke, was invited to organise a tour to Australia by the Melbourne Club for the 1887–8 season. It was formed in the face of a rival tour invited by various Sydney dignitaries and began badly when Hawke had to return to England on the death of his father. The teams played several times against the same opposition and even combined as a united England side for one "Test Match". Both tours were a financial disaster for hosts and visitors alike, with James Lillywhite, one of the backers, defaulting on his debt.

***Stop the Seventy Tour* poster
(1970)**
**Acquired by MCC
at auction, 2011**
After the Cricket Council
indicated that the 1970
South African tour of England
would go ahead in April, the
Government of Harold Wilson
pressured it to withdraw the
invitation. The activities of
the Stop the Seventy Tour
campaign, led by Peter Hain,
had threatened to disrupt the
visit and resulted in an attack
on the Lord's pitch which
was subsequently put under
24-hour guard. The additional
threat of a boycott of the
approaching Commonwealth
Games in Edinburgh by African
and Asian countries enraged
the South African authorities,
who said the cancellation
amounted to "a total disregard
for sport and the rights of
others".

**Scorebook from the Hastings Cricket Festival, 1886**
**Acquired by MCC at auction, 2011**

This scorebook records one of the matches on the groundbreaking tour by the Parsees, the first representative Indian side to play in England. Their tour began at Sheffield Park (see p.116) and ended at Cumberland Lodge, Windsor Great Park in a match organised at the express desire of Queen Victoria and featuring Princes Victor and Albert. The Parsees specifically requested that W.G. Grace be included in the MCC team to play them at Lord's, and he scored 65 and took 11–44. They recorded only one victory during their trip but perhaps this is unsurprising given the team comprised enthusiasts who were willing and able to fund their trip.

*played at Hastings on Monday & Tuesday the 19 & 20th of July 1886*

**SECOND INNINGS OF The Parsees**

| | STRIKER. | SCORE. | TOTAL | HOW OUT. | BOWLER. | REMARKS. |
|---|---|---|---|---|---|---|
| 1 | M. Framji | 22 | 4 | Bowled | Kidman | |
| 2 | A. C. Major | 1114243144434 32344/1111 | 49 | not out | | |
| 3 | M.P. Banajee | 11 | 2 | run out | | |
| 4 | J. M. Morinas | | 0 | C & B G Chichester | A. Clarke | |
| 5 | D. Khambatta | 1121 | 5 | Bowled | Kidman | |
| 6 | S. N. Bhedwar | 41211 | 9 | " | " | |
| 7 | B. Balla | 4411 | 10 | " | " | |
| 8 | B. Baria | 34441 | 13 | " | " | |
| 9 | P. C. Major | 11 | 2 | C & B J.J. Oliver | A. Phillips | |
| 10 | J. D. Pochkhana | 12 | 3 | C & B G Chichester | Kidman | |
| 11 | A. K. Libuwalla | | 0 | Bowled | " | |
| | Byes | 2233 | 10 | | | |
| | Leg Byes | 112/1 | 6 | | | |
| | Wide Balls | 11 | 2 | | | |
| | No Balls | | | | | |
| | | TOTAL | 115 | | | |

**RUNS AT THE FALL OF EACH WICKET.**

| For 1 | For 2 | For 3 | For 4 | For 5 | For 6 | For 7 | For 8 | For 9 | For 10 |
|---|---|---|---|---|---|---|---|---|---|
| 5 | 7 | 9 | 21 | 69 | 87 | 108 | 111 | 115 | 115 |

**ANALYSIS OF THE BOWLING OF THE SECOND INNINGS.**

| | BOWLER. | RUNS FROM EACH OVER. | WIDE BALLS. | NO BALLS. | RUNS. | WICKETS. | OVERS. | MAIDEN OVERS. | BALLS BOWLED. |
|---|---|---|---|---|---|---|---|---|---|
| 1 2 3 | Kidman | M! .w MM; .M! ./! ..w 42 :Mw .4! ./ .4.w .3 4! . /..7 :M! !MM 2.wMM.w | | | 39 | 7 | 27 | 10 | 108 |
| 4 5 | A. Clarke | :..MM.M! ..2. :M! 4MM! .2 M! 4M 3 3/.7 MM! .3 .MM. 4 M | | | 33 | 1 | 23 | 13 | 92 |
| 6 | J. Parkin | :. 4754 | 1 | | 15 | 0 | 3 | 0 | 13 |
| 7 | D. G. Laugham | MMM 43 | | | 7 | 0 | 4 | 3 | 16 |
| 8 9 10 11 | A. Phillips | /!. :! :M! :. MMMM | 1 | | 7 | 1 | 9 | 5 | 36 |

ENTERED AT STATIONERS' HALL.
W. H. & S.

**West Indians in the Players' Dining Room, 2009**
**Photographed by**
**Graham Morris**
The West Indian team arrived in England for a curtailed tour of two Test Matches and three One-Day Internationals that lasted only twenty days in total. It replaced the Zimbabwe team, whose tour had been cancelled following a directive from Prime Minister Gordon Brown. The conduct of elections in Zimbabwe had been questioned and Britain followed South Africa in severing its cricketing ties. The team are pictured in the Players' Dining Room during the lead-up to the match as part of series of "Behind the Scenes" photographs commissioned from Graham Morris by *The Times* newspaper.

*MCC v New Zealand* by Gill Lancaster (1937)
Published by London Transport, acquired by MCC at auction, 2005

In 1908 Frank Pick was appointed to take over publicity for the London Underground and immediately recognised the unfulfilled potential of this powerful medium. Although he initially worked with an established commercial designer, he was not content to work with printing firms, and directly commissioned artists and illustrators – some established, others only beginning their careers – with stunning results (see also p.169). The 1937 tour saw more draws than results but was notable for the Test debuts of Len Hutton and Denis Compton, while New Zealand fielded three "Double All Blacks", men who have played both cricket and rugby for New Zealand; there have been seven in all.

MCC v. NEW ZEALAND AT LORD'S
MAY 12 AT 2.30   MAY 13 & 14 AT 11
By UNDERGROUND to ST. JOHNS WOOD

**Watercolours from the sketchbook of Tom Coates Commissioned by MCC, 2000**

When MCC first pursued the idea of sending artists to tour with the England Test team, it decided in the first instance to commission an established artist. Tom Coates was trained at the Royal Academy Schools in the early 1960s and has subsequently been President of the New English Art Club and the Royal Society of British Artists. His sketchbooks are filled with images of the fateful tour of 2000, which featured the infamous declaration by South African captain Hansie Cronje who was later accused and found guilty of match-fixing. These sketches were subsequently worked up into a selling exhibition of pictures at Lord's. Its success set a precedent and allowed MCC to commission younger, more untried artists to tour during the next decade.

**Kodak Camera belonging to A.P.F. Chapman, 1920s**
**Donated to MCC by Mrs Wendy Weston, 2011**

Percy Chapman, England captain between 1926 and 1931, made his Test debut before ever playing county cricket. He was appointed captain for the decisive last Test of the Ashes tour of 1926 and that victory heralded eight more, a record that still stands. This assured him immediate fame and popularity with the public but, as with many players, he perhaps took more comfort being the other side of the camera. He was one of many cricketing tourists, some provided with cameras and film by commercial companies, who recorded life on the road. From "Hopper" Read and Percy Fender to Alec Bedser, Trevor Bailey and Alan Oakman – and now of course Graeme Swann.

**Selection of Cricket Balls including that gifted to Patsy Hendren, 1921**
**Donated to MCC by Hendren, 1954**

Patsy Hendren joined the Lord's groundstaff aged sixteen and debuted for Middlesex in 1909. He still holds the third highest first-class career runs aggregate behind Jack Hobbs and Frank Woolley. Nicknamed Patsy because of his Irish heritage, he was a gregarious character; his obituary in *Wisden* recounted: "No game in which he was engaged could be altogether dull. If it looked like becoming so, Hendren could be relied upon at one time or another to produce some antic which would bring an appreciative chuckle from the onlookers. Furthermore, he was a first-rate mimic and wit, qualities which made him an admirable member of teams on tours."

**Silver-mounted emu egg presented to William Burrup by Spiers and Pond (1882) Donated to MCC by Mr J. Treacher, 1946**

This egg was presented to William Burrup by the Melbourne firm of Spiers and Pond for the part he played in the arrangement of the first tour by an English team to Australia in 1861. The firm had originally hoped to entice Charles Dickens to present a series of readings, but when he declined they looked to cricket to provide the financial solution. The 1859 tour to the USA had proved a successful precedent and the growing popularity of cricket in Australia was borne out by the tour. Burrup was a founder member and Secretary of Surrey CCC and seven of the tourists were Surrey men.

**Commemorative poster designed and illuminated by J.G. Attwood**
**Donated to MCC by Grand Metropolitan plc, 1995**

At the base of the poster are roundels listing all of the matches played on the 1861–2 tour of Australia. As was the custom, and because of the relatively low quality of the opposition, the England side played against teams of 22 to even out the odds. None of these matches was considered first-class, but there was one such contest staged at the Melbourne Cricket Ground, in which H.H. Stephenson's team split: the Surrey players, joined by five "Surrey" locals, were defeated by the "World XI".

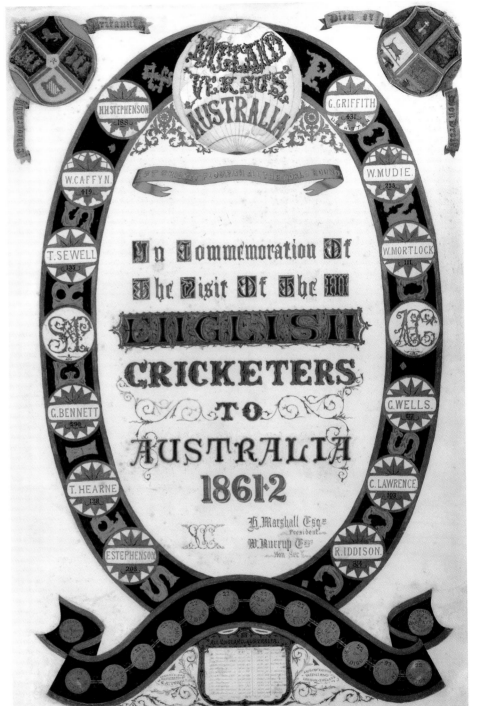

# All India

Though the first team from India toured the UK in 1886, it was only in 1932 that the first All India team arrived. The outstanding player was C.K. Nayudu, who scored over 1500 runs, including a century during the match against MCC at Lord's, and was chosen by *Wisden* as a Cricketer of the Year in 1933. The team was captained by the Maharajah of Porbandar although he stood aside, in favour of Nayudu, for the one Test Match – the first ever played by an Indian team.

Inaugural Pataudi Trophy presentation at The Oval, 2007. Captain Rahul Dravid and "Tiger" Pataudi (seated front)
Photographed by
Tom Shaw, 2007
The trophy was commissioned from Jocelyn Burton by MCC.

**William Gunn bat used by C.K. Nayudu, 1932**
**Donated to MCC by Miss Chandra Nayudu, 1982**
C.K. Nayudu hit a century at Lord's against MCC on this, the first tour by "All India" in England.

It was another aristocrat who laid the foundations for India's first series victory in England in 1971 under the captaincy of Ajit Wadekar. According to Sunil Gavaskar, "Tiger" Pataudi "liberated Indian cricket" through his demeanour and batting style. Bishen Bedi said he was "the first captain to give us a feeling of Indian-ness". He is celebrated at Lord's in the trophy commissioned in 2007 by MCC to celebrate the 75th anniversary of All India tours. It was presented that same summer to captain Rahul Dravid on the third occasion that an Indian side has won a series in England.

Dravid made his Test debut at Lord's in 1996, falling agonisingly short of a century; he made up for this with an undefeated century on his last appearance at Lord's in 2011, averaging 76 for the series. Despite this, India, World Test No. 1 and World Cup Champions, failed to win a single international match on the tour.

The other captain to win a Test series in England was the great all-rounder Kapil Dev in 1986. This followed the astounding World Cup Final victory at Lord's in 1983 which, some argue, changed the course of Indian cricketing history. The match hinged on the dismissal of Vivian Richards, as described by Gideon Haigh: "The crowd on the midwicket boundary began shrinking back; even Father Time ducked … Kapil Dev turned, ran back with the flight of the ball, loose stride eating up the distance, cast a split-second glance over his shoulder, and collected the descending ball in his fingertips – making even this look deliberate. Has a more difficult catch been made to seem easier at a more critical moment in the annals of the game?"

The Museum offices are situated behind the Pavilion and have absorbed the viewing balcony to the real tennis court which used to be reserved for ladies – they were not allowed to spectate from the dedans. Once a spectator dropped a handbag from that balcony on to the penthouse, resulting in not only an explosion of makeup and lipstick but a delay in play, while the marker retrieved a ladder to clear the court.

The marker's voice is one of the sonorous (in most cases) rhythms of the day as he adjudicates the sometimes feisty handicap contests between competitive Members. On major cricket match days he is of course silent, and instead the noises of the crowd drift in through the windows, alerting us to events on the field, tantalisingly out of sight in front of the Pavilion. Should the radio, television or even internet commentary happen to be on, then there is a slow ripple of exclamations, with the arrival of a wicket or the heralding of runs echoing from one commentary to the next, ending with the television replay action. Sometimes it is a contrasting silence, a pause in the natural hum of the crowd, that tells the story.

On occasions the clear-cut signal is muddied by the delayed reaction of stragglers in the Harris Garden catching sight of the action on the proliferation of smaller screens around the Ground. Later may come a jeer or slightly muted roar as the spectators respond to a replay on the screens, and later still the umpiring decision confirmed or contradicted by the DRS system.

Most of the statistics broadcast are now fed digitally from the scorers esconced in their cramped if tailor-made box, square to the wicket below Father Time. Their records are now completed without the aid of pens, pencils or felt pens so beloved of statisticians from Bill Frindall to Irving Rosenwater, who each in their own style painted a pointillist scene on their score sheets. It is more akin to the original days of cricket when scorers notched their score sticks from their perch on the boundary edge or, as some early illustrations would have it, from a blanket of coats thrown down within the outfield.

Scorers have been an almost permanent presence, an integral part of the early game. They were included within cricket's "exact representation" by artists such as Boitard and Hayman, in the ribald satires of Rowlandson, the topographical prints of cricket scenes, the "Laws" handkerchiefs and later broadsheets. In still

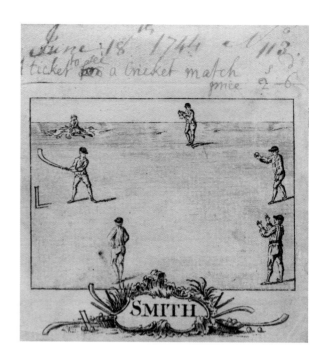

**Ticket for a cricket match, 1744**
**Donated to MCC by Julian Marshall, before 1907**
The ink inscription dates the ticket to 18th June 1744, with a price of 2s 6d.

Previous pages: Eighteenth-century cricket bats in the Writing Room, donated by the 6th Duke of Buccleuch. These are some of the earliest cricket bats in the MCC collections. They are stamped with makers' marks at a time when specialist craftsman were only just emerging.

later scenes they actually take centre stage, given the difficulties of depicting on-field play and the attraction of the boundary edge to genre scenes by such artists as John Ritchie, John Robertson Reid and Carl Werner, to name but three.

The most obvious and fine example is that depicting William Davies, scorer to the Lewes Priory Cricket Club and Sussex County, as depicted by a local artist Thomas Henwood (p.118). He is pictured in 1842, the year he died, and is surrounded by the tools of his trade: his pen and scoring notebooks, the equipment for the match and a Chesterman tape measure for setting out the creases at the start of play. As Robin Simon writes, "this ritual … was not handed over to the groundsman (and thus incorporated into the laws) until later". One of his actual scorebooks from 1832 still exists in the collection, and it is evocative to recall William Slatter's depiction of Mr Knight, who, although not a scorer, performed much the same role as the only recognised newspaper representative of the time, writing for *Bell's Life*:

> [He] stood all day in the bushes inside the rails [of the Pavilion], this being the only place from which to view the cricket on a crowded day, with no scoreboard or cards to tell him the state of the game, and having to record the whole of the score of the match in his own score-book …

John Arlott would no doubt have approved of the hob-nob goblet, and that, in spite of this obvious refreshment, the accuracy of his scorebook was unaffected. Arlott in fact was a great enthusiast for the picture, thinking it to have the finest "character" of any early "cricket" painting.

Scorers continue to feature in late Victorian images such as John Robertson Reid's *Country Cricket Match* as part of the boundary spectators, and their influence is also felt indirectly in the largest picture at Lord's. This depicts a match between players of the Marylebone and Melbourne Clubs who never actually played together but who were considered, presumably on the basis of their statistics,

**The MCC (Melbourne) team by Robert Ponsonby Staples (1887)**
This is one half of the pendant picture to *An Imaginary Cricket Match at Lord's* by Robert Ponsonby Staples and George Barrable (see pp.20–1, 28)

T. W. GARRETT · P. S. McDONNELL · S. P. JONES · A. C. BANNERMAN · H. J. H. SCOTT · F. R. SPOFFORTH · G. GIFFEN · G. E. PALMER · J. McC BLACKHAM · W. L. MURDOCH · G. J. BONNOR

to be the finest players of their generations. It does seem that by the time Lord's current Ground was up and running, these statistics, in the shape of scorebooks, were an established part of the game. James Pycroft, admittedly writing 40 years after the event, recalled the fact that not all the MCC records had been destroyed in the Pavilion fire, for some had been stored at Thomas Lord's house. William Slatter included mention of them in his description of the scorers' perch at Lord's:

> The scoring … was done on a stand made of iron rods framed up with a wooden seat and back, about seven feet from the ground. The scorers rested the scorebooks on their knees and if the rain came suddenly they often got wet with their book, before they could scramble down from their perch and seek shelter under the old sheds, where the Grand Stand now stands. The scoreboard was attached to this stand on the right hand, and the scorer on that side also had to put up the figures.

Whether or not those same scorebooks mentioned by Pycroft and Slatter have endured to this day is not clear, although the Club can boast a truly singular set of scores by its first official scorer, Samuel Britcher. Every year from 1790 to 1805, he produced a set of materially insubstantial but historically hugely important volumes entitled *A List of All the Principal Matches of Cricket that have been Played in the Year* (p.175).

For many years, thanks to the generosity of Lady Julien Cahn, MCC owned several volumes from this series; then in 2009, thanks to the offices and research of David Rayvern Allen, the only known volumes for years 1790–94 were secured from the Hammond family to complete the set. John Hammond was an old wicketkeeper for Sussex, whose son Charles also played for the county. The family corresponded with many of the great collectors from Ashley-Cooper and A.L. Ford (see chapter 7) to Alfred Gaston, and it was his great-great-grandson who passed the books to Lord's.

The books themselves are carefully bound together into one volume and those who have handled them can understand why. They are the most insubstantial of pamphlets and fit into the category of ephemera rather than books. Overlooked by all but the most

**Australian batting order, Third Test v England, 1930 Acquired by MCC, date unknown**

# Order of going in.

### FIRST INNINGS.

1  Woodfull
2  Jackson
3  Bradman
4  Kippax
5  McCabe
6  Richardson
7  a'Beckett
8  Oldfield
9  Grimmett
10  Wall
11  Hornibrook

discerning collectors, such throwaway items often have minimal financial value (though not in this case!) but can provide a wonderful accent on an event or its chronicler. The batting order of the 1930 Test at Leeds, written in the captain's hand, is an immediate reminder of an old-fashioned duty undertaken by a captain. Equally the doggerel verses of Albert Craig, the "Surrey Rhymester", capture the flavour of a hawker in amid a cricketing crowd.

Britcher's immediate successor was William Denison, the first secretary of the Surrey Club who reported cricket for *The Times* in the 1840s, worked on *The Sporting Magazine* and wrote a number of works, not least *The Cricketers' Companion* (reproduced in facsimile by MCC, as were Britcher's scores).

At the same time on the other side of the Atlantic, Henry Chadwick began reporting cricket for *The New York Times*. Ten years later he was converted to baseball, persuaded that it was better suited to the American temperament. That said, he always maintained a high regard for cricket, believing its "interminable" delays to be a custom in violation of the Laws of the game. He is best known for devising the baseball box scoring system that, with few amendments, is still in use today; as a result his portrait hangs in Baseball's Hall of Fame in Cooperstown, New York.

However, perhaps the natural heir to Britcher, both in terms of historic value and connection to MCC, is Arthur Haygarth. He became the most noted historian of the early game by dint of his fifteen volumes of *Scores and Biographies* covering a period from the 1740s to the 1890s. The work was initially published by Fred Lillywhite, but MCC subsequently took on the costs and hold the manuscripts, in addition to a collection of his books and papers from the Cahn library donated in 1944.

As his epic work came to a close in the final few years of the nineteenth century, the first dedicated press facilities were set up at Lord's. They suffered an inauspicious start: reported as far too limited and rough and "altogether unworthy of Lord's", they were destroyed not long afterwards in a storm. Perhaps the contemporary scoreboxes suffered the same fate, for MCC set out in its annual report of 1905 that it would expand the professionals' pavilion to provide permanent accommodation for the press.

This presumably was the accommodation about which E.W. Swanton wistfully reminisced in *Daily Telegraph* in 1958, believing himself to be the last writer to leave the press box

> where the game has been written about for half a century ... So passes the old box where the Pardons reigned supreme, where one remembers as a young man being

appropriately awed by Charles Stewart Caine, where Neville Cardus at first was too shy to enter.

Swanton wrote this after the press moved to the Warner Stand, which included much better facilities, although the angle for viewing was far less satisfactory. In *The Boundary Book* (1962), Robin Marlar, himself a press man after his playing career, described the position of the scorers then in his description of the Grandstand:

> The great scoreboard is its centre piece. From a "Bridge" above it the notchers peer down; and theirs is probably the best view of all. The scoreboard seldom lets the public down, and when it does its efforts to right itself are greeted with jeers. If the cat-callers could only see the chaotic mass of bands and wheels behind its impeccable face, they would be silent, for the strangeness of the machine is made even more grotesque by its size.

One who would certainly have joined the cat-callers was the author, statistician, editor and MCC Member Irving Rosenwater. At the first auction I attended on behalf of the Club, he stood up and berated the auctioneer as a vandal for splitting up bound volumes of collected scores, and he was a meticulous keeper of records with a "mania for veracity and accuracy". When he died, his papers weighed over 40 tons and included everything from annotated drafts of his book manuscripts to mint condition MCC membership cards (exchanged for his used ones at the end of every season) to his original scoresheets for both the BBC and Kerry Packer's World Series. The latter have found a home at Lord's and, along with other papers and correspondence, shed fascinating light, from his very particular perspective, on the opposing poles of the cricketing globe.

As a BBC scorer both he and Bill Frindall would have retained their positions in the Pavilion as part of the broadcast media, though the official scorers lost their position in the Grandstand on its replacement in the mid-1990s. They were temporarily reunited with the press in the Warner Stand before being recompensed with their current position, directly under the stumps of Father Time, when the new digital scoreboards were repositioned at the end of the 1990s.

It was not the press themselves but the ICC who were responsible for their final relocation to the imposing J.P. Morgan Media Centre of today. The World Cup Final's return to Lord's in 1999 prompted the ICC Chief Executive to emphasise the requirements of at least 200 journalists and broadcast media who would be arriving. It was Tony Lewis, himself a broadcaster as well as a former England captain, who represented the view at the MCC Committee that any new facility should be behind the bowler's arm.

The Media Centre is an architectural tour de force. Dramatically stylish, its angled glass face diminishes glare, while its pale blue interior renders it neutral to the players' eye. In this last respect, for all its technology and futuristic design, it seems all the same to have been pre-empted, though the writer of this letter to *The Times* in 1936 suspected different motivations altogether:

Sir, Various explanations have been put forward to account for the lack of success which has attended Oxford (and Harrow) at Lord's in recent years. Some observers have attributed this to luck of the toss or otherwise. There is however an explanation which I have not yet seen advanced. I refer to the sinister fact that the inside of the scorer's box at Lord's is painted light blue. This is obviously an insuperable obstacle to the success of any dark blue side, but whether it is due to caprice or prejudice on the part of the scorers, or the MCC authorities, has not been revealed to me.

**Advertising Poster by Felix Topolski, published by London Transport (1938)**
**Acquired by MCC, c.2005**

# The Voice of Cricket

John Arlott, original member of the *Test Match Special* team, handed over to Christopher Martin-Jenkins after his last TMS commentary during a match at Lord's in 1980. Christopher, in his well-chosen following remarks, hoped that he was launching a happy retirement rather than ending a great career. For many CMJ took up Arlott's commentary baton, though sadly he himself was not able to realise the retirement he had wished on his preddecesor, dying in 2013 at the age of 68.

*Test Match Special* broadcasting from the Media Centre, Lord's, 2007 Photographed by Graham Morris
The window frame of the TMS box was specially cut into the glass elevation of the Media Centre in order to allow microphones to pick up the noise of the crowd.

**The *Test Match Special* team meet Queen Elizabeth II in the Committee Room, 2001 Photographed by Patrick Eagar**
Peter Baxter, Henry Blofeld, Jonathan Agnew and the late CMJ and Bill Frindall receive a cake in the best of TMS traditions.

Christopher broadcast for almost 40 years as part of the TMS team and in his final years played a significant role at Lord's, becoming MCC President, a fitting tribute to his multi-faceted contribution to the game. Adam Mountford, the programme's producer, remembered him in two light-hearted moments from broadcasting spells at Lord's:

"He was unbelievably forgetful. During a Lord's Test he asked me if I could leave him off the rota before lunch as he had been invited to the England and Wales Cricket Board Chairman's box. I duly did so, only to be surprised to see him queuing for food in the Media Centre later. "Wasn't the lunch any good in the box?" I asked him. "What box?" he said. "The Chairman's box," I replied. CMJ then let out a stream of his famous "non-swear words" and ran to the other side of the ground.

"If there is one moment of which I will think most fondly about CMJ it will be when he got the fit of the giggles at Lord's in 2009. It started as an innocent spell of commentary on a match against New Zealand: 'Broad's in, he bowls, this time Vettori lets it go outside the off stump, good length, inviting him to fish,' he said. However, the giggles came only seconds later as he went on to describe Vettori's response: 'But Vettori stays on the bank ... and keeps his rod down, so to speak.' At that point, sniggers could be heard in the commentary box from myself and others as CMJ tried in vain to regain his composure. 'I don't know if he is a fisherman, is he?' he said as his voice got higher, struggling to stifle his laughter."

**South African Cricket uniforms including those of Shaun Pollock, Dale Steyn and Hansie Cronje**
**Loaned to and acquired by MCC, 2004–12**

South Africa has a proud reputation at Lord's, winning its first Test in England and consequently its first series in 1935. Since the international ban (1970–91) was lifted, the United Cricket Board's team has never lost in Lord's Tests (see p.59). Perhaps the most remarkable indivdual performance was that of Geoff Griffin in 1960. The *Daily Mirror* reported "a volcanic crescendo of excitement" as Griffin, No-balled for throwing eleven times, still bagged the first and only hat-trick in a Lord's Test. The match ended early and an exhibition game was hastily arranged in which he was No-balled for changing to bowl underarm without notifying the umpires. He was immediately consoled by Donald Bradman but never played Test cricket again.

**Portrait of Muttiah Muralidaran by Phil Hale**
**Commissioned by MCC, 2007**

This artist worked with Murali for over an hour in the nets in Cambridge during the Sri Lankan tour. The finished work is nevertheless unresolved, reflecting the consternation that his action caused to cricket authorities. Like Geoff Griffin, who had an accident in childhood, he had a flexed elbow (in his case congenital), but when he was called for throwing in Australia the issue was re-examined by the ICC. This resulted in a change to the Laws allowing a greater degree of flexibility in a bowling action; despite this he continued to be heckled by Australian crowds, whereas Griffin was greeted with warmth and sympathy during his time in England.

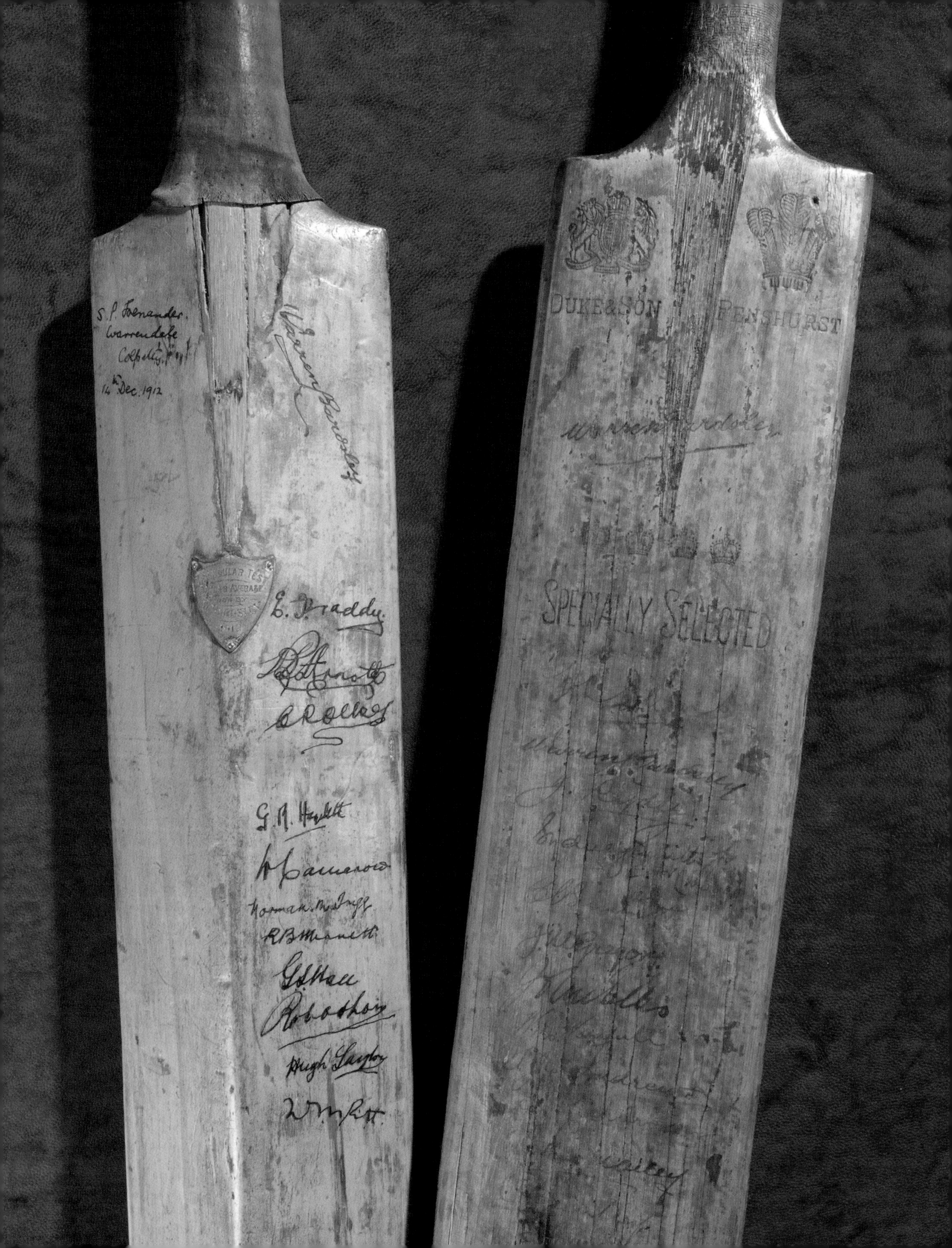
DUKE&SON
PENSHURST
SPECIALLY SELECTED

**Cricket bats belonging
to Warren Bardsley, 1912
and 1926
Donated to MCC by
S.P. Foenander, 1953,
and acquired from
Don Oslear, 2004**

Warren Bardsley is a relatively unsung hero of Australian cricket, though his tours to England were particularly successful. In 1909 he had a poor string of scores until the final match when he became the first man to score a century in both innings of a Test. In 1912 he was the leading run scorer in the famous triangular series with an average over 60. After the First World War he continued playing but his form deserted him, and it was somewhat surprising that he was chosen to tour again in 1926, aged 43. Not only did he have to assume the captaincy because of illness, but he made 193 at Lord's, carrying his bat – the oldest Australian to score a Test century.

**Signed England shirts
Donated or loaned to MCC by
the players, 2004–12**

Photographed in the Home Dressing Room at Lord's, these match-worn shirts (and one very long pair of trousers!) reflect not only wonderful performances by individuals at Lord's – Ashley Giles, Monty Panesar, Stuart Broad, Andrew Strauss, Alastair Cook and Jonathan Trott – but the growing success of the England team over the last decade. The shirts show the subtle variations – sponsors' logos aside – that have been added to the plain white Test shirts: the commercial logo rather than original crest with royal approval, individual player numbers, individual series embroidery and, with a change of kit manufacturers, the introduction of bright white rather than the traditional cream or off-white tone.

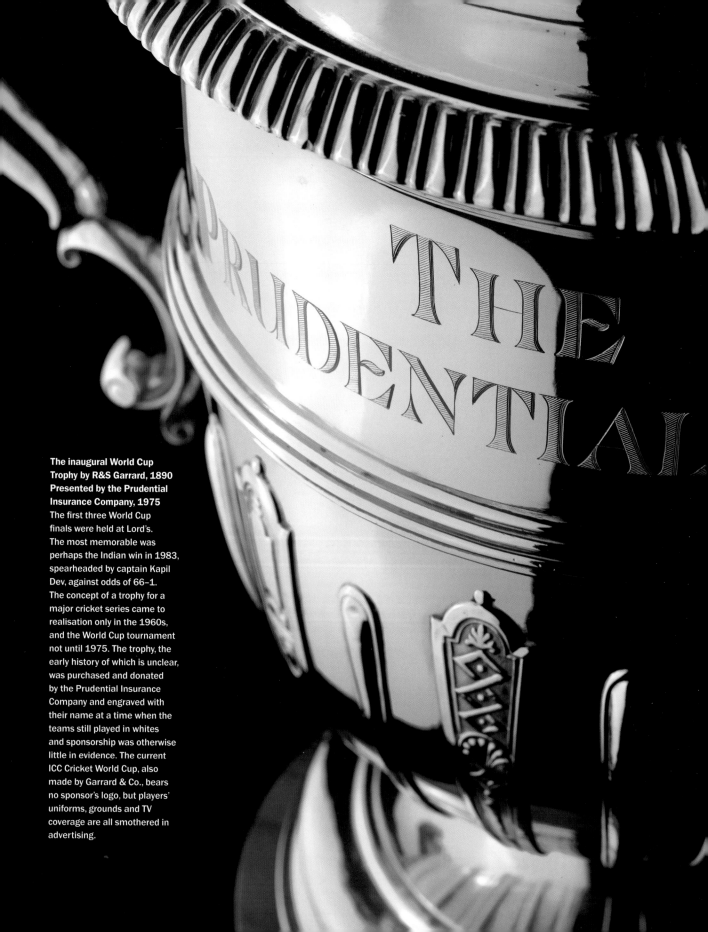

**The inaugural World Cup Trophy by R&S Garrard, 1890 Presented by the Prudential Insurance Company, 1975**
The first three World Cup finals were held at Lord's. The most memorable was perhaps the Indian win in 1983, spearheaded by captain Kapil Dev, against odds of 66–1. The concept of a trophy for a major cricket series came to realisation only in the 1960s, and the World Cup tournament not until 1975. The trophy, the early history of which is unclear, was purchased and donated by the Prudential Insurance Company and engraved with their name at a time when the teams still played in whites and sponsorship was otherwise little in evidence. The current ICC Cricket World Cup, also made by Garrard & Co., bears no sponsor's logo, but players' uniforms, grounds and TV coverage are all smothered in advertising.

# ENGLAND v. ALL-INDIA

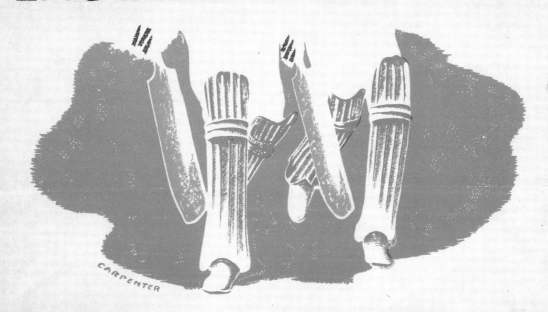

# AT LORD'S • JUNE 27, 29 & 30

STATION : ST. JOHNS WOOD

BUSES: 2 · 13 · 23 · 23ᴮ · 48 · 53 · 74 · 121 · 153

COACHES: H1 · H2 · K1 · K2

36/1650/46.000  36.1652.23,000

The Baynard Press

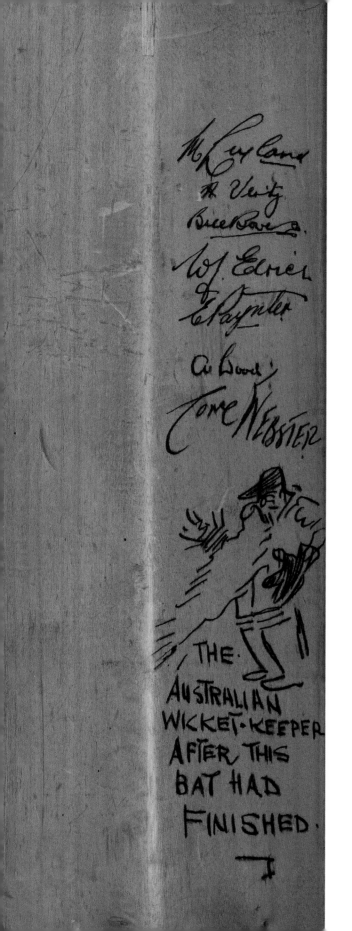

**Gradidge bat used by Len Hutton, 1938**
**Donated to MCC by Sir Leonard and Lady Hutton, 1956**

Sir Leonard Hutton was the first professional player to captain England and arguably its finest batsman. He was the archetypal Test player who, as the cartoon suggests, ground out his runs, occupying the crease for long periods. His then world record score of 364, beating the triple centuries of both Hammond and Bradman, was achieved at The Oval against Australia with this bat, in an innings of over thirteen hours. The team declared on 903, another record for that time.

**The Gillette Cup, designed by Alex Styles, made by Garrard & Co., 1963**
**Presented by Gillette Company, 1963**

The Gillette Cup, the limited-overs knockout competition which was part of English county cricket from 1963 to 1980, broke new ground not only in its cricketing format but also in the commercial sponsorship of cricket trophies. The modern commercial aspect was balanced in the trophy's design by the use of the Father Time motif. This combination of innovation and tradition mirrors the development of Lord's itself.

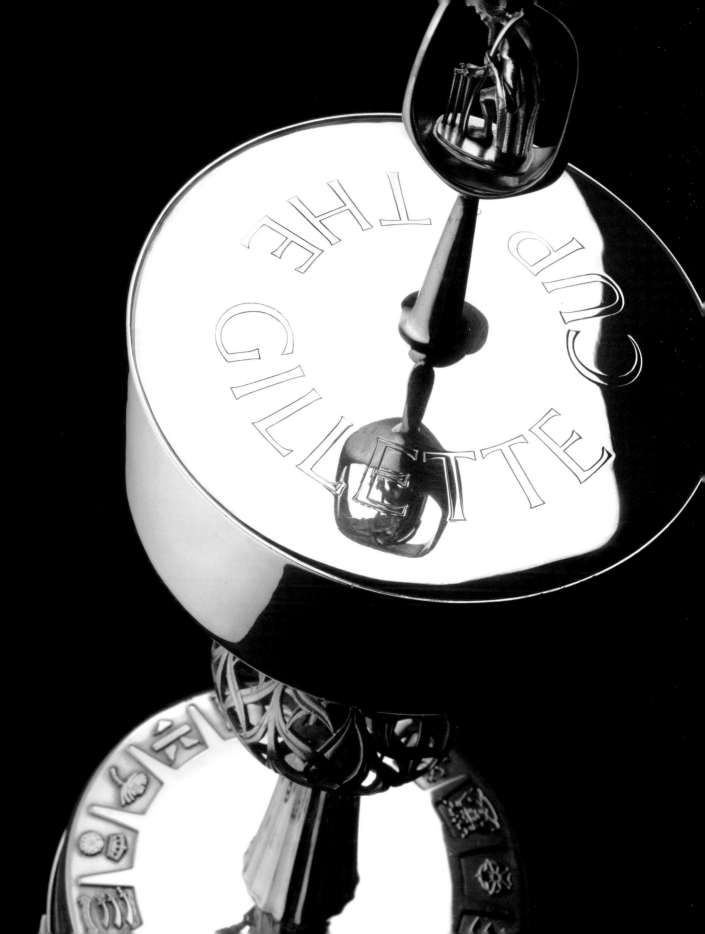

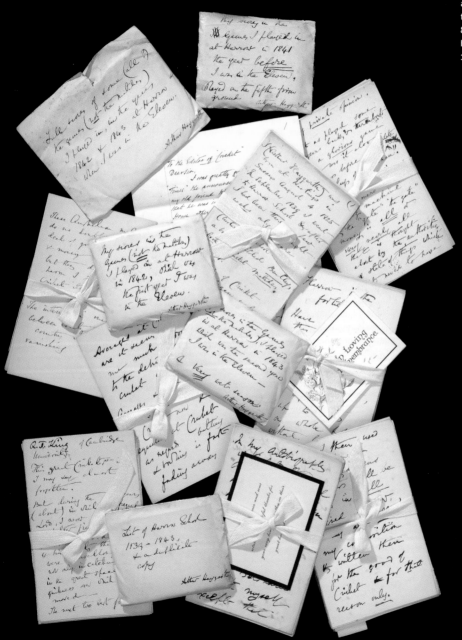

*Scores and Biographies* by Arthur Haygarth, 1854–74 Acquired by MCC from the author, c.1874, and part donated by Lady Julien Cahn, 1944

Among the most important contributors to cricket history was Arthur Haygarth, who was born within days of the fire at Lord's that engulfed all of the club's records in 1825. While his predecessors published information on scores and dismissals, Haygarth prepared both match records and also a wealth of information about the players; he covered over 8500 matches and over 3000 biographies for the years 1744–1878.

**World Twenty20 and One-Day International shirts Donated to MCC by the players, 2003–11**

In the last decade one of the major priorities for the Lord's collections has been to reflect international cricket stars of recent years in all forms of the game. These shirts represent some of the most characterful of these players: Kevin Pietersen, man of the series as England won their first major championship in 2010; Shahid Afridi, who captained Pakistan to victory in the ICC World Twenty20 at Lord's in 2009; Sourav Ganguly, the steely Indian captain whose shirt-swinging celebrations on the players' balcony caused consternation as his side chased down over 300 in an ODI at Lord's in 2002; and Kumar Sangakkara, whose impassioned MCC Spirit of Cricket Cowdrey Lecture in 2011 received a standing ovation but caused political controversy in Sri Lanka.

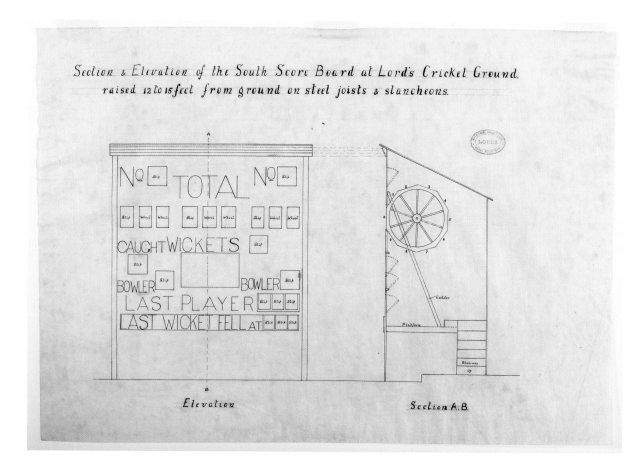

*Section & Elevation of the South Score Board at Lord's Cricket Ground.*
*raised 12 to 15 feet from ground on steel joists & stancheons.*

*Elevation*

*Section A.B.*

**The South Score Board at Lord's, date unknown**

The year 1846 saw the introduction of the first telegraph scoreboard at Lord's, which showed runs, wickets down and the score of the last man out. Two years later the printing tent appeared and the public bought detailed scorecards for the first time. The telegraph system was employed for 150 years before it was finally superseded by digital scoreboards, which rapidly gave way to replay screens that show the score. A subtle difference perhaps, but it is clear that these boards are now very much part of the game, rather than reflecting it: DRS decisions, replays, player statistics may all actually influence the game in progress.

The most important of the early recorders of the game was Samuel Britcher. He was official scorer for MCC at Lord's and, although his series of scores from 1790 to 1805 seems limited by today's standards, it was the first attempt to publish cricket records in an annual form. Individual volumes of his work have survived in very limited numbers and the only complete extant run of his work is conserved in the MCC Library collection.

**Cricket bat used by
Albert E. Trott, 1902
Donated to MCC by
Mr R. Binns, 1943**

Trott is the man responsible for one of cricket's most famous big hits, launching the ball over the Pavilion at Lord's – the only man to have done it – off Monty Noble in 1899. He was awarded four runs only, as the ball was not hit out of the Ground. Two months earlier he had straight-driven Sussex's Fred Tate into one of the turrets which top either end of the pavilion, credited by some as a much bigger hit. Others have come close: Keith Miller in one of the 1945 Victory Tests, Mike Llewellyn in the Gillette Cup final in 1977, Kim Hughes in the Centenary Test of 1980, and Kieron Pollard in the Twenty20 championship in 2010. For the 2011 season Marcus Trescothick was offered £1 million by his new bat sponsors (who named their new bats after Trott) if he managed to clear the Pavilion, to no avail.

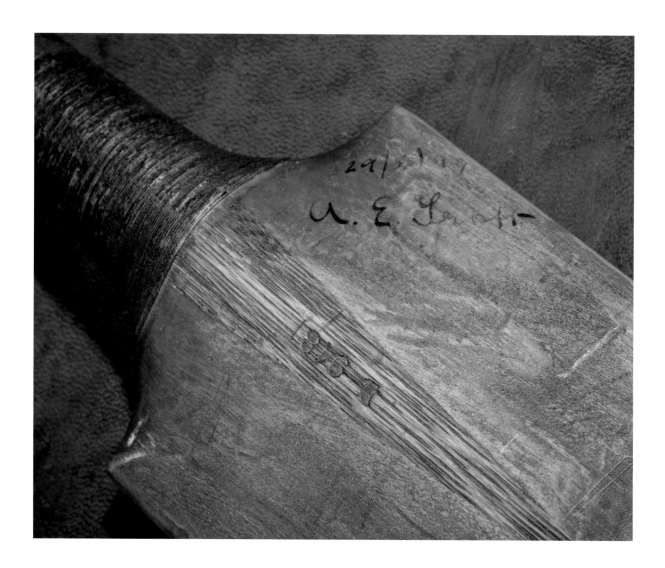

**Australian Cricket Team v
All England, Sydney Cricket
Ground, 1895
Photographed by Osborne
Brothers, donated to MCC
by E.A. Humphreys, date
unknown**
Trott (seated second from right)
is one of the enigmas of late

nineteenth-century cricket.
He made his debut during this
tour by England and followed
up bowling figures of 8 for 43
and innings of 38 and 72 not
out in Adelaide with 85 not
out in Sydney, where he was
not asked to bowl! Despite his
average he was not selected

for the 1896 tour to England,
captained by his brother, but
made his own way to England
and there played for Middlesex
and MCC against Australia
(see opposite). He toured with
England to South Africa in
1898–9 and took 17 wickets at
an average under 12.

# Spin Kings

Shane Warne, Murali and Kumble: none of them took five wickets in an innings here. Who then can claim to be the kings of spin at Lord's? Surprisingly, perhaps, there has been a steady stream of English wicket-takers. Swann, Illingworth and Peebles; Lock, but not Laker; Nick Cook on debut, Ashley Giles and Monty Panesar – all have taken five. Yet, "Tuffers" aside, no such joy for Middlesex men. No Titmus, Emburey or Edmonds (though the latter's 4 for 6 off 8 is hard to beat).

**Derek Underwood, photographed by Patrick Eagar, 1974**
"Deadly" took eight second-innings wickets and thirteen in the match in this Test against Pakistan at Lord's.

How have the visitors fared? Five-wicket hauls for Vettori, Mushtaq and Bob Holland of Australia. The masters of Indian spin Bishen Bedi and Bhagwat Chandrasekhar grafted for their places on the honours boards, together conceding over 350 runs for their wickets. But only one visiting spinner has taken a ten-for: twenty-year-old Sonny Ramadhin took 11–152 when he and his spin "twin" Alf Valentine bowled West Indies to their first ever victory over England in 1950. The celebration calypso "Cricket Lovely Cricket" was appropriately composed and recorded by the popular Lords, Kitchener and Beginner!

England's finest spin performances, bar one, came in the time of uncovered pitches. The country's preeminent leg-spinner Doug Wright (1947) and off-breaking Roy Tattersall (1951) clinched record hauls against South Africa and Johnny Briggs (1886) against Australia. They are overshadowed by Hedley Verity, whose fifteen wickets in 1934 sealed England's only Ashes victory of the twentieth century. He was not to return from the war, but his memory lives on at the ground at which he played more times than any other.

When it comes to ten wickets in a match, only one bowler has "done the double", and he did so after pitches became that much less conducive to the spinner's art. In 1969 "Deadly" Derek Underwood cracked New Zealand with 30 minutes left to play (rain was to wash out the impending final day). Five years later, he was sent a helping hand when water leaked under the covers; the rain returned once more but this time to save Pakistan, despite his thirteen wickets.

**Prize cricket balls of Hedley Verity, Writing Room**
**Acquired by MCC from Douglas Verity, 2012**
These balls include one of those used in the Ashes Test at Lord's in 1934 when Verity took a record fifteen wickets.

# 7.
# What Do They Know of Cricket ...

When Diana Rait Kerr took over the curatorship in 1945, the "bulk of the library [was] packed away in lockers". Wartime precautions had dictated its removal from the modest space within the Pavilion, today described as the "Old Library" (see p.112). It comprised one major collection, that of Alfred Lawson Ford, a serious collector of cricket memorabilia from his teens until his death at the age of 80 in 1924. His library was originally bequeathed to Alfred's nephew, Hugh R. Ford, who subsequently presented it to MCC in 1930.

As a book collector he was very selective, eschewing annuals and periodicals entirely, but his collection, while not as extensive as some – amounting to no more than 800 volumes by the time of his death – was notable for including much of the rarest and most valuable printed material on the subject of cricket. His collection of artworks was rather more extensive. When Alfred J. Gaston wrote about Ford's collection in 1905, it already numbered more than 5,000 prints and paintings, many of them mounted in a series of massive and expensively bound scrapbooks. In later years Ford shunned modern prints, concentrating exclusively on older

**A.L. Ford scrapbooks,
Writing Room
Donated to MCC as part of
the A.L. Ford Collection by his
nephew Hugh R. Ford, 1930**

material, and his bookplate symbolises the art of collecting to highly selective criteria.

The second major donation came in 1944, upon the death of Sir Julien Cahn, though his collection needs to be prefaced with a note on Frederick Samuel Ashley-Cooper (1877–1932), another lifelong collector of books and pictures, but also a noted scholar on the history of the game and its foremost statistician. In a life devoted to cricket Ashley-Cooper assembled a collection of over 4,000 books and pamphlets, spanning well over 200 years of the game's history and covering the total geography of the cricketing world. He was a less selective collector than Ford, refraining only from acquiring duplicate copies. He understood Ford's preference, given the practical limitations of space, but contended that many annuals, especially those from certain Australian associations which contained a breadth of detail, were essential to the understanding of the history of cricket in a particular location.

This is a key point in understanding Ashley-Cooper's collection, as it was the library of a working historian. Ashley-Cooper was editor of and a contributor to *Cricket: A Weekly Record of the Game*, and compiled, edited or wrote over 100 books and pamphlets himself. His collection contains many of the manuscript notes which preceded each published volume as well as his personally annotated copies of the publications themselves.

Shortly before Ashley-Cooper died, his friend A.W. Shelton persuaded Sir Julien Cahn to take the collection "lock, stock and barrel" for his large house, Stanford Hall in Nottinghamshire. The Ashley-Cooper volumes then formed the backbone of Cahn's library and, though this library was an adjunct to his other cricketing activities, Cahn did supplement it with items from other renowned collections, such as that of Robert Stratton Holmes, who died a few months after Ashley-Cooper in 1933.

Following Sir Julien's sudden death in 1944, his vast collection was dispersed, in circumstances which today are still not completely understood. His granddaughter Marina Rijks in her biography *The Eccentric Entrepreneur* attempts to explain:

> Lady Cahn offered the MCC the opportunity to select any item it did not already possess. As it was wartime … the Club could not send a representative and instead chose a local Nottingham firm to act on its behalf. It was Ashley-Cooper's set of books that was chosen. Unfortunately due to the haste with which the selection was carried out, it was later discovered that the Lord's collection contained about half of the Haygarth and half of the Ashley-Cooper sets substantially diminishing the value of the gift.

Somewhere, a private collector had the balance. E.E. Snow, writing in 1964, pointed out that ownership of the Ashley-Cooper set morally resides with MCC and it was to be hoped that the collector in question would honour this in due course. Unfortunately this was never to be the case.

Happily, of the great number of books and pamphlets that were presented to MCC, the majority have an Ashley-Cooper provenance, including many unique manuscripts or annotated works.

These major bequests have naturally attracted many further smaller, individual offers and perhaps none more symbolic than that of E.W. Swanton's copy of the *Wisden* Almanack for 1939 (p.195). Though it contains no annotations in the style of Ashley-Cooper, its personalisation is distinct thanks to its wartime popularity among Swanton's fellow prisoners-of-war and its wryly humorous reference to "Foster & Gould Bookbinders" in Nakawn Paton, Thailand, in 1944.

Such experiences do seem to have played out long ago and far from the lives of most of today's professional cricketers, and yet the game persists in reflecting much of the social history of what is now an increasingly small world.

**Imran Khan by Emma Sergeant (c.1985)**
**Acquired by MCC at auction, 2004**

The artist first met the cricketer in 1982 and sketched and painted him several times. Imran returned most recently to Lord's to deliver the Cowdrey Lecture in 2010.

Though not specifically a literary event, the annual Cowdrey Lecture presents an individual's viewpoint on the state of cricket. It was established in honour of Lord Cowdrey in 2000, at the time when a preamble on the Spirit of Cricket was added to the Laws by MCC. Distinguished speakers have included top cricketers such as Sunil Gavaskar, Clive Lloyd and Martin Crowe, but perhaps the most affecting have been those whose experiences or speeches have gone far beyond cricket: Imran Khan, Desmond Tutu and most recently Kumar Sangakkara, whose speech on his team's attack by terrorists and the travails of his homeland brought a standing ovation, huge press coverage, and censure from the Sri Lankan authorities.

The title of this chapter is taken from a quotation from the historian and writer C.L.R. James, who himself adapted it from Rudyard Kipling's words "What do they know of England, who only England know". Regularly cited as one of the great sports books of the twentieth century, C.L.R. James's *Beyond a Boundary* (1963) is, by his own famous definition, about far more than cricket. Developing a concern to understand sport as part of a much wider social and political context, James's study is part autobiography, part historical study and part political call-to-arms written against the backdrop of the decolonisation struggles. His reflections thus reach out into a critical account of racism and imperialism, into wider questions of aesthetics and popular culture, and into the struggle for revolutionary social change, which was the enduring concern of his life. Crucially, James insisted that such questions were not simply of concern to academics or to experts, but were also a central part of what drew ordinary men and women to sport.

When James first arrived in London to co-author a book at the invitation of the great cricketer Learie Constantine, he wrote for the *Manchester Guardian*. Throughout that period the paper's cricket correspondent and chief music critic

**Dinner invitation on the occasion of the publication of W.G. Grace's *Cricket* (1891)**
Lord's regularly hosts publishing events including the annual launch of the *Wisden* Almanack, and launches a Sports Literary Festival in 2013.

was Neville Cardus (see p.198). Described by John Arlott as the "creator of modern cricket writing", Cardus always maintained that his reporting was secondary to his central focus in life, namely music. Christopher Brookes, in his biography, includes a letter to the *Sydney Morning Herald* while Cardus was working in Australia:

> Mr Cardus's phrasing and diction are music itself, and his comments so graphic that one lives and moves for the time being in the scenes and situations associated with the music, and the composer becomes a living presence.

How equally that could refer to his cricket writing.

Although one might not describe the broadcaster John Arlott's dulcet tones as musical, they were unmistakeable and his diverse interests – poet, policeman, prospective MP and wine connoisseur – informed his commentary to enrapture everyone from Desmond Tutu to John Paul Getty (both listened while convalescing and consequently became lifelong cricket fans). I was introduced to Shahryar Khan, President of the Pakistan Cricket Board and one-time Foreign Secretary, at a match at Lord's and an effortless six prompted him to quote Arlott: "the stroke of a man knocking a thistle top off with a walking stick".

The nephew of the editor of *Punch* may not have been as poetic as Arlott but he certainly captured the Zeitgeist in 1882, in response to England's tumultuous defeat by Australia. It stunned the public and provoked considerable criticism in the press. Two days after the match a first humorous obituary appeared, punning on the name of England's last man (see p.194), an example which was then followed by *The Sporting Times* whose journalist Reginald Brooks penned the more famous notice:

> In Affectionate Remembrance of English Cricket which died at the Oval … R.I.P. … N.B. The body will be cremated and the ashes taken to Australia.

Why was this latter preferred? It can only have been for its reference to the heated debate raging in English society about the practice of cremation, whose legitimacy was still being questioned at that time. Brooks's father was a prominent supporter of the Cremation Society, set up in 1874 to advocate and legalise the cremation of human remains. The matter came to a head in October 1882 when Captain Hanham, denied official permission by the Home Office, erected a crematorium on his own estate and burnt the bodies of his wife and mother. On this occasion the authorities took no action but the following year Dr William Price was arrested for attempting to cremate the body of his five-month-old son. At his trial in February 1884, the judge pronounced cremation legal, a decision that was ratified by an Act of Parliament in 1902.

The power of the press has then played a full part in the promulgation of the story of the Ashes, and the home of the Urn also supports a great tradition of printing too. Scorecards were first championed at Lord's by Fred Lillywhite from a tent pitched on major match days. This became a printing "box", and when the new Grandstand was constructed in 1866 a dedicated print "shop" was provided. This expanded in line with Club needs and was finally moved under the Mound Stand in the redevelopment of the 1990s. Geoffrey Moorhouse in 1983 wrote:

**England vs MCC & Ground Scorecard from Lillywhite printing tent, 1834**
**Donated to MCC as part of the Ford Scrapbooks, 1930**
The printing department at Lord's still continues Lillywhite's tradition to this day.

Vince Miller … and his two accomplices produce ⌈scorecards and⌉ much else that MCC requires ⌈under the Grandstand scoreboard⌉ … This wouldn't be worth remarking were it not for the fact that everything … has been entirely hand set. Inside the place resembles any small jobbing printers' shop with its high tilted working benches, its metal formes ⌈sic⌉, its mallets, its inky smell … Caxton would recognise those three instantly, from their ways of working.

The archive of their work preserves a flavour of the changing social life of Lord's, a fascinating supplement to the records of the business of cricket contained within the Club's precious minute books. When taken together, this treasure trove of documents and the wealth of literature contained within the MCC Library illustrate as nowhere else the breadth and depth of cricket writing, and indeed the variety and richness of character of the sport's authors.

# Lord's Gospel

Known as the "Little Wonder", John Wisden came from one of two great cricketing families of the nineteenth century (the Lillywhites were the other). Although a great all-round cricketer, with his name on the trophy contested by West Indies and England since the 1960s, his true legacy is the little yellow "bible" of cricket, published annually in April at a dinner in the Long Room, with its authoritative statistics, the cream of cricket writing and formidable editorial. In 2013 the *Wisden Cricketers' Almanack* celebrates its 150th edition.

*Cricket at India Gate, Delhi, photographed by Clive Mason, 2011*
This was one of the shortlisted entries for Wisden MCC Photograph of the Year 2012

## The Cricketer's Bible

Alec Waugh in *The London Mercury*, c.1938

Towards Christmas there came, as always there must come, an evening when we sat over the fire and remembered suddenly that it was four months since we had held a cricket bat, that May was still a long way off … On such an evening we take down *Wisden* and pore over the old scores long after our usual bedtime. For *Wisden* is the cricketer's bible. The uninitiated make mock. What is it, they say, but a record? We can understand your wanting to look up the scores of matches you have seen that will recall to you pleasant hours in pleasant company. But what possible enjoyment can you get out of reading figures and accounts of matches that you have never been to? … It is hard to explain. In the same way that the letters x and y possess a significance for a mathematician, so for the cricketer these bare figures are a symbol and a story. We can clothe the skeleton with flesh. We can picture the scene. We know exactly how it happened. We know what the score-board looked like when the seventh wicket fell, we can gauge the value of Strudwick's 5 not out, and when we read 'Ducat lbw b. Woolley 12' we know exactly the emotion of the man sitting at the end of the free seats below the telegraph. If only Ducat can stay in, he had thought, Surrey may win yet … And as we study the figures of Warner's many centuries, we are sitting again on the mound, looking into that haze which covers the ground shortly after five o'clock in August, with the sun blazing on to us from the left of the pavilion, and to shield our eyes we have bent the match card beneath our hats."

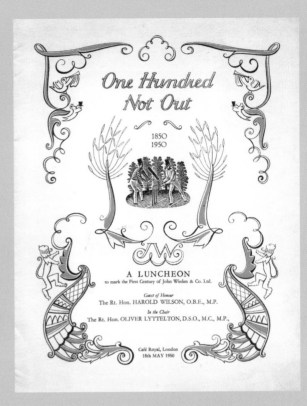

**Menu from *Wisden* centenary luncheon, 1950**
**Bequeathed to MCC by**
**E. Rockley Wilson, 1957**

***Lord's Cricket Ground* by Robert Seymour (1833) Donated to MCC by G.S. Layard in memory of Abel John Layard, 1920**

John Nyren was the son of Richard Nyren, captain of the famous Hambledon Club during its eighteenth-century heyday. The younger Nyren was not a distinguished cricketer, but he made his own contribution to the game in later life, working with Charles Cowden Clarke to produce a series of histories called *The Cricketers of My Time*. Then in 1833 a series was collected and published together with an instruction manual called *The Young Cricketer's Tutor*. It remains a classic of early cricket literature and this is the original drawing for its frontispiece.

**The United England XI by John Corbet Anderson (1852) Donated to MCC by Ethel Slatter, 1955**

The United England XI were one of the two rival touring sides of the nineteenth century, formed by a disgruntled John Wisden and James Dean (see pp.138–9). Here they are pictured either side of Fred Lillywhite's printing tent which produced scorecards "under the patronage of MCC". Lillywhite travelled with the England touring team to the USA and Canada in 1859, bringing his own printing press and scoring tent, which travelled with the team. In unpredictable weather it often caused problems on coaches and trains, to the extent that his captain lost patience and left him and his press behind with instructions to catch up later. Once at the ground, however, the tent was a main attraction and it issued updated scorecards throughout the matches.

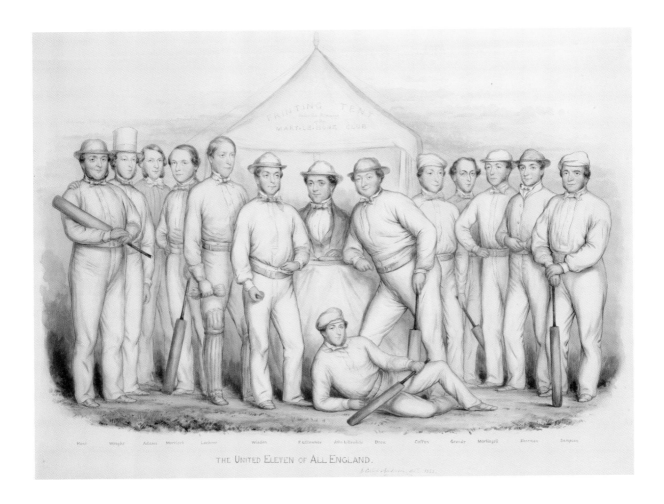

THE UNITED ELEVEN OF ALL ENGLAND.

**The diary of R.E. Foster**
**Donated by C.K. Foster, 1971**

R.E. Foster was a member of the first MCC team to tour Australia in 1903–4 and kept this hand-written journal as a record of the trip. He describes not only the story of the tour but the particular experience of scoring 287 at Sydney, the highest individual score by any player to that date: "… & in an hour and ten minutes put on 130 for the last wicket before I was caught at cover by Noble off Saunders – Rhodes being 40 not out – the total was 577 which is the highest ever made …"

**The original manuscript of W.G. Grace's *Cricket* (1891) Donated to MCC by L.D. Brownlee, 1925**

Grace's book is a curious blend of subject matter, an indication that the public, enthralled by his personality and celebrity as much as his on-field prowess, were keen to read the great man's writings on every aspect of cricket. The book set the template for celebrity cricket books which continues to this day, not least in its being ghost-written. The original manuscript is in the hand of Grace's friend and biographer W. Methven Brownlee.

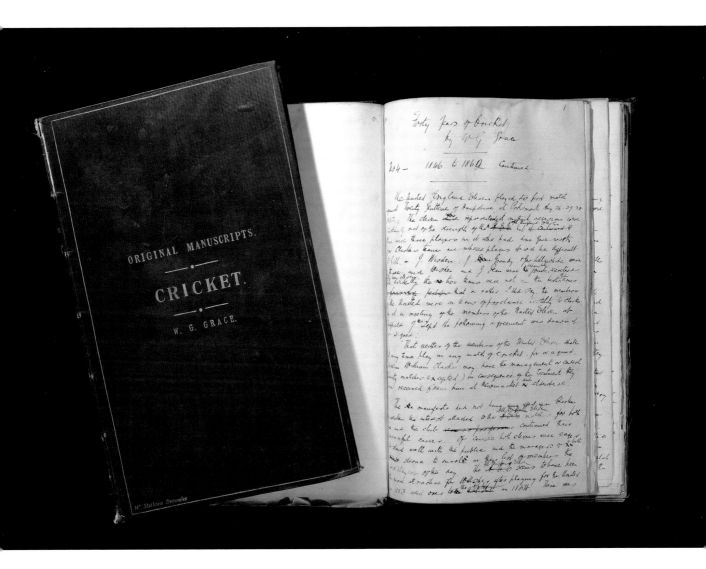

## ONDON PRICES.

FRIDAY NIGHT.

### KSHIRE HANDICAP.

DAY, SEPTEMBER 12.
(urlongs 132 yards.)

| lb | Taken | | Offered |
|---|---|---|---|
| 13 ... | 9 to 2 | ... | 9 to 2 |
| 6 ... | 7 to 1 | ... | 7 to 1 |
| 10 ... | 7 to 1 | ... | 7 to 1 |
| 12 ... | 7 to 1 | ... | 7 to 1 |
| 11 ... | 8 to 1 | ... | 8 to 1 |
| 4 ... | 8 to 1 | ... | 8 to 1 |

### . LEGER.

DAY, SEPTEMBER 13.
(urlongs 132 yards.)

| Taken. | | Offered. |
|---|---|---|
| 6 to 4 | ............ | 6 to 4 |
| 9 to 4 | ............ | 2 to 1 |
| 0 to 1 | ............ | 10 to 1 |
| 0 to 8 | ............ | 10 to 1 |
| 3 to 1 | ............ | 33 to 1 |
| 3 to 1 | ............ | 33 to 1 |
| 0 to 1 | ............ | 40 to 1 |
| | ............ | 50 to 1 |
| 6 to 1 | ............ | 50 to 1 |
| 0 to 1 | ............ | 100 to 1 |
| | ............ | 100 to 1 |
| | ............ | 100 to 1 |
| | ............ | 100 to 1 |
| | ............ | 100 to 1 |
| | ............ | 100 to 1 |
| | ............ | 100 to 1 |
| | ............ | 100 to 1 |
| | ............ | 100 to 1 |
| | ............ | 200 to 1 |
| | ............ | 200 to 1 |
| | ............ | 200 to 1 |

### RBY, 1883.

| Taken. | | Offered. |
|---|---|---|
| 0 to 1 | ............ | 10 to 1 |

### REWITCH.

BER 10. (2 miles 2 furlongs 8 yards).

| lb | Taken. | | Offered. |
|---|---|---|---|
| 5 ... | 20 to 1 | ... | 20 to 1 |
| 0 ... | 20 to 1 | ... | 20 to 1 |
| 2 ... | 25 to 1 | ... | 25 to 1 |
| 4 ... | 25 to 1 | ... | 25 to 1 |
| 6 ... | 25 to 1 | ... | 25 to 1 |
| 0 ... | 25 to 1 | ... | 25 to 1 |
| 3 ... | 25 to 1 | ... | 25 to 1 |
| 2 ... | 33 to 1 | ... | 33 to 1 |
| 2 ... | 33 to 1 | ... | 33 to 1 |
| 0 ... | 33 to 1 | ... | 33 to 1 |
| 2 ... | 33 to 1 | ... | 33 to 1 |
| 3 ... | 33 to 1 | ... | 33 to 1 |
| 2 ... | 33 to 1 | ... | 33 to 1 |
| 0 ... | 40 to 1 | ... | 40 to 1 |

### IDGESHIRE.

CT. 24 (1 mile 240 yards).

| lb | Taken. | | Offered. |
|---|---|---|---|
| 6 ... | 25 to 1 | ... | 25 to 1 |
| 6 ... | 25 to 1 | ... | 25 to 1 |
| 6 ... | 33 to 1 | ... | 33 to 1 |
| 6 ... | 33 to 1 | ... | 33 to 1 |
| 6 ... | 33 to 1 | ... | 33 to 1 |
| 4 ... | 33 to 1 | ... | 33 to 1 |
| 3 ... | 50 to 1 | ... | 50 to 1 |

e first nursery of the year. you !

nough, a drum took first youngsters. Mr. Walker

again, and is becoming unters' flat races. When

SNELLING AND MORGAN are very much wanted, and Sackville Street Myers will give a pony a-piece for their apprehension and conviction.

To Members of Parliament, journalists, diners-out, and others :—
"Mr. Gladstone must not be contradicted, as it is bad for his health." So the edict has gone forth. The other evening at a dinner party one of the guests disagreed with the Premier on some point that turned up, and a warm discussion ensued in which the right honourable gentleman displayed all the command of language, temper, and manners that distinguishes him alike in public and private life. The combat had raged for about five minutes, when Mr. Gladstone's opponent was handed a slip of paper on which were pencilled in Mrs. Gladstone's handwriting the words :—
"Mr. Gladstone must not be contradicted, as it is bad for his health."

"THE second ought to have won," persisted Gubbins.
"Very likely," said Barney; "but then you see, old man, unfortunately for you 'oughts' don't count."
"The deuce they don't!" said Nathaniel. "I only wish Master would add an ought or two to the meagre cheque he weighs in with on a Saturday."

A SPORTSMAN there was in the Blues
Who hied to the banks of the Ouse;
He plunged upon Friday,
And cried, "This is *my* day !
They told me the horse couldn't lose."

*Ab ovo usque ad mala.* Free translation by T'owd Mon—From the Oval to the champagne.

BILLY WRIGHT, Joe Davis, and Harry Morris have bought a yacht. Billy is to be captain, Harry steward, and Joe cook !

---

In Affectionate Remembrance
OF
ENGLISH CRICKET,
WHICH DIED AT THE OVAL
ON
29th AUGUST, 1882,
Deeply lamented by a large circle of sorrowing
friends and acquaintances.

R. I. P.

N.B.—*The body will be cremated and the
ashes taken to Australia.*

---

HOORAY ! The *Daily Telegraph* has had a correspondent on the "armoured train," and he has discovered that the authorities have furnished the sailors with flint and steel weapons ! At least, this is the only way by which we can account for the description of a Jack Tar *priming* his rifle. A traveller says he knows this armoured train well. It starts from Baker Street and goes to Ramleh or Hornseh, he forgets which.

UNDER the title of "The Broads and Rivers of Norfolk," an interesting and useful little guide to the country about Norwich has been issued, which we recommend to our readers.

THE *Bird*, in setting Tommy Bowles right about the name of the Speaker's residence, informs him that "Glynde is a picturesque village eight or nine miles from Brighton on the London Road." Now, if Tommy were

**E.W. Swanton's *Wisden Cricketers' Almanack*, 1939 edition**
**Bequeathed to MCC by E.W. Swanton, c.2000**
Unique among *Wisdens*, this one was kept by the well-known author and commentator for 3½ years while working on the Burma to Siam railway as a Japanese captive during the Second World War.

Lovingly rebound several times with tattered remnants of gas cape, held together with rice paste, it bears a Japanese stamp to indicate that the book was considered "non-subversive". As a result of constantly circulating among his fellow prisoners, it has a claim to being the most widely read copy of *Wisden* ever.

**Authors v Artists,
photographed by
H. Vandyck, 1903
Acquired by MCC,
date unknown**
The Authors club that played
its last match in 1912 was
a wonderful combination of
literary talents. It played an
irregular series of matches
against other teams of

actors, publishers and artists,
including one against the
Press Club at Lord's in 1896.
The club was reincarnated in
2012 and its first season of
fixtures – each carefully chosen
as representative of an aspect
of cricket – is celebrated in a
book, with chapters assigned
to individual writers.

AUTHORS v. ARTISTS.—May 22nd, 1903.

E. W. Hornung   E. V. Lucas   P. G. Wodehouse   J. C. Snaith   G. Chowne   Sir A. Conan Doyle   Hesketh Prichard   L. D. Luard   C. M. Q. Orchardson   L. C. Nightingale   A. Kinross

C. Gascoyne   Shan F. Bullock   G. Hillyard Swinstead   Reginald Blomfield   Hon. W. J. James   A. E. W. Mason   E. A. Abbey   A. Chevallier Tayler   J. M. Barrie   G. C. Ives   G. Spencer Watson

H. Vandyck.                                                                                      130. Ladbroke Grove. W.

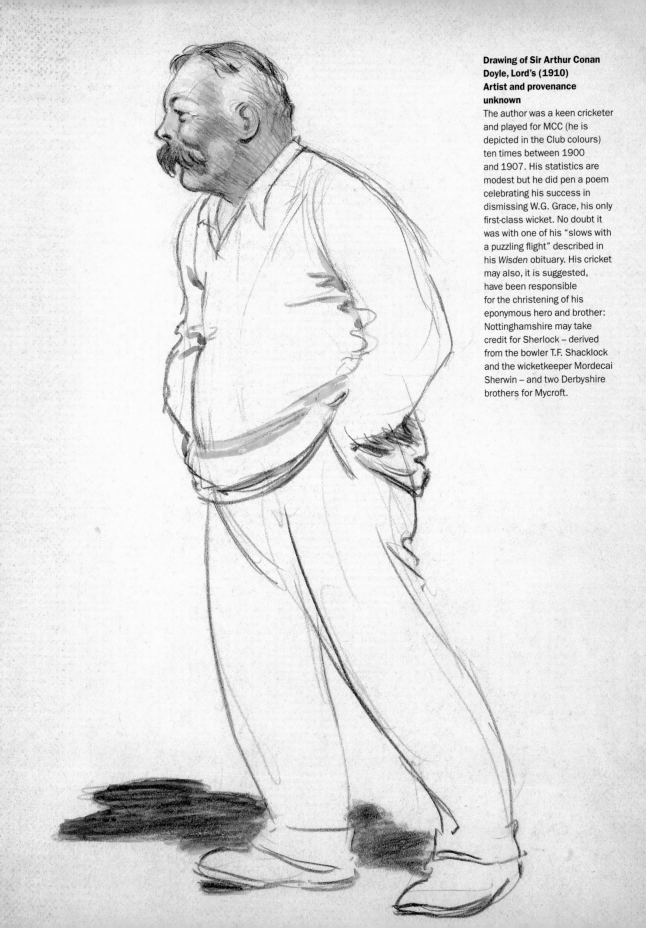

**Drawing of Sir Arthur Conan Doyle, Lord's (1910)**
**Artist and provenance unknown**

The author was a keen cricketer and played for MCC (he is depicted in the Club colours) ten times between 1900 and 1907. His statistics are modest but he did pen a poem celebrating his success in dismissing W.G. Grace, his only first-class wicket. No doubt it was with one of his "slows with a puzzling flight" described in his *Wisden* obituary. His cricket may also, it is suggested, have been responsible for the christening of his eponymous hero and brother: Nottinghamshire may take credit for Sherlock – derived from the bowler T.F. Shacklock and the wicketkeeper Mordecai Sherwin – and two Derbyshire brothers for Mycroft.

**The Dream of Cardus**
**Artist, date and provenance unknown**
Neville Cardus was both music critic and cricket correspondent for the *Manchester Guardian* from the late 1920s and, having spent time in Australia, worked for the *Evening Standard* as well as writing for the *Sunday Times*. Though untrained in music, his talent for personal, vivid and romantic criticism helped transport him, in the eyes of both music and cricket fans, to much more than a mere reporter. Indeed it was to him that *Wisden* turned in 1963 for his choice of the Giants of the Wisden Century: he went for Sydney Barnes, Sir Donald Bradman, W.G. Grace, Sir Jack Hobbs, Tom Richardson and Victor Trumper. Never an establishment man, he faced some opposition in his candidacy for MCC membership, but was knighted for his work in 1967.

**John Arlott and Keith Miller in the BBC Radio Commentary box at Lord's**
**Photographed by Patrick Eagar, 1980**
Policeman, poet, prospective MP, wine connoisseur, journalist and author, John Arlott brought all to bear in his wonderful commentaries on cricket. A devotee of Cardus, he was lauded for his own turn of phrase: countless gems such as "Botham runs in like a shire horse cresting the breeze". The Centenary Test between England and Australia was John Arlott's final Test as a BBC commentator and it signalled the end of a career which started in 1946. His final words were "… and after Trevor Bailey, it will be Christopher Martin-Jenkins". When his retirement was announced there was a spontaneous ovation from both crowd and players.

**Cricket Match between Dingley
Dell and All Muggleton**
**Print of the design for the back
of the £10 note (1991–2)**
This design succinctly
encapsulates the essence of
nineteenth-century cricket.
With the link to Dickens the
man, it tips a wink to cricket's
first trip to Australia in which
the English team were second
choice to a possible lecture
tour by the author (see p.150).

As an illustration for a bank
note, it acknowledges the
palpable motivation behind
so much early cricketing
activity. Finally, extracted from
a Dickens novel (*The Pickwick
Papers*), it symbolises the
place of cricket in a wonderful
range of fiction from Siegfried
Sassoon and P.G. Wodehouse
to Douglas Adams and Joseph
O'Neill.

**Bowled!!** **by Mervyn Peake (1951)**
**Inscribed "For Kit", acquired at auction by MCC, 2005**
As artist, poet, illustrator and novelist Mervyn Peake represented a wonderful combination of talents. His creativity and imagination are manifest both in his *Gormenghast* books and in his graphic images for works by Lewis Carroll, Samuel Taylor Coleridge, the Brothers Grimm and Robert Louis Stevenson. This quirky and personal cartoon, an unusual find, perfectly exemplifies the original humour to be extracted from on-field action, whether it be through word or picture, and whether or not one is an aficionado of the game.

## IMPERIAL CRICKET CONFERENCE.

A meeting of the Imperial Cricket Conference was held at Lord's on Tuesday, July 20th, 1909, at 4.30 p.m.

**Present.** Lord Harris (in the chair); and Lord Hawke (representing M.C.C.), Messrs. P. A. MacAlister and L. O. S. Poidevin (Australia), and Messrs. A. Bailey and H. D. G. Leveson-Gower (South Africa).

**Minutes.** The minutes of the last meeting were read by the Chairman and signed as correct.

**Rules for Test Matches.** Rule 2, which had been deferred, was altered to read as follows:—"A Cricketer who has played in a Test Match for a Country cannot play for any other Country without the consent of each of the contracting parties." These rules were recommended for adoption. (See A herewith)

**Umpires in Test Matches.** Umpires in Test Matches shall be selected by a Committee equally representative of each country.

**Hours of play in Test Matches.** The hours of play shall be the usual hours for Test Matches in England; with a ten interval according to the practice in force in Inter-County Cricket.

**Visit, Triangular Cricket Contest.** A scheme for an interchange of visits between England, Australia and South Africa, including a Triangular Cricket Contest, in 1912 was approved. (See B herewith)

**Arrangements.** A scheme for the arrangements under which a Triangular Cricket Contest should be played was approved. (See C herewith)

### A.

## RULES
## FOR TEST MATCHES.

1.—Test Matches are those played between Representative Elevens of England and of Australia and of South Africa, also between Elevens of Australia and South Africa.

2.—A Cricketer who has played in a Test Match for a Country cannot play for any other Country without the consent of each of the contracting parties.

3.—Qualification by Birth.—A Cricketer, unless debarred by Rule 2, is always eligible to play for the Country of his birth.

4.—Qualification by Residence.—A Cricketer, unless debarred by Rule 2, may elect to play for any Country in which he is residing and has resided for not less than the 4 years immediately preceding and thereafter shall always be eligible to play for that Country.

### B.

## Suggested Programme
OF
## INTERNATIONAL GAMES
BETWEEN
## England, South Africa & Australia.

MAIN PRINCIPLES:—

(1) No team from any Country shall pay visits in two successive seasons.

(2) Each such team shall pay a visit to and receive a visit from each other Country in every Cycle of four years.

### Table showing practical working of above.

| YEAR. | MONTHS. | COUNTRIES MEETING. | NEXT ROUND. | |
|---|---|---|---|---|
| 1909 | May to August | Australia in England | 1913 | |
| 1909-10 | November to March | England in South Africa | 1913-14 | |
| 1910 | May to August | | 1914 | |
| 1910-11 | January to March | South Africa in Australia | 1914-15 | |
| 1911 | May to August | South Africa in England | 1915 | |
| 1911-12 | November to March | England in Australia | 1915-16 | |
| 1912 | May to August | Triangular Contest | 1916 | |
| 1912-13 | March to April | Australia in South Africa | 1916-17 | |

N.B.—In view of the Triangular Contest in 1912 South Africa defers its visit in 1911 to 1912, and Australia's visit in 1913 is advanced one year to 1912.

### C.

## Scheme for Imperial Cricket Contest.

1.—England, Australia and South Africa shall play each 6 Test Matches in England, each playing the other 3 matches.

2.—Each Country shall take one-half of the gross gate taken at the Test Matches in which it takes part. The net proceeds of Stand Money to be pooled for the benefit of the Ground on which the match is played and the Counties.

3.—Each visiting team shall in addition to Test Matches play, if possible, at least one match with each First Class County, and with the M.C.C.

4.—The Board of Control shall fix the dates of the Test Matches before July 31st, 1911, to enable the County Secretaries to make their programmes without undue inconvenience.

5.—(a) For the purpose of providing for complimentary and other stand tickets, each contesting party shall receive 100 free stand tickets and shall have the option of purchasing 500 additional stand tickets for each Test Match, at the current rates, and that no other provision shall be made in this respect. Such option to be exercised at least 14 days before the match for which the tickets are required.

(b) For the convenience of accurately ascertaining the amount of gate money to be divided, the sale of stand tickets shall in no case include the entrance fee to the ground.

6.—That not more than three days be allotted to each match.

7.—(a) The price of admission to all Test Matches shall be 1/-

(b) The price of admission to all matches, other than Test Matches, shall be arrived at by arrangement between Australia, South Africa and the local authorities on whose grounds such matches are played.

**Laws of Cricket (c.1740)**
**Donated to MCC by Colonel**
**R.S. Rait Kerr, 1939**
The earliest known Laws
of Cricket date from 1727
and formed a private written
agreement between two
gentlemen who had organised
two cricket matches between
their own teams. The sixteen
articles did not provide full
details of how to play cricket
and were evidently set down
to provide clarity in areas of
likely dispute. In 1744 a code
of Laws was agreed, but it
was not until 1752 that it was
printed on paper, published and
distributed widely. The earlier
examples of the 1744 code
were printed on decorative
handkerchiefs such as that
pictured.

# From Our Own Correspondent

John Woodcock, MCC Arts and Library Committee member, and correspondent of *The Times* for over 50 years, is perhaps the most notable chronicler of modern times. Departing from his cottage in Hampshire, occupied by only three Woodcocks since 1814, he covered fourteen tours to Australia. His first four (1950–1 to 1963–4) involved a month's passage from Tilbury to Fremantle, cheek by jowl with the team. His articles are therefore well-informed, hugely evocative, and cover an unparalleled period. Owing to his self-deprecating nature, no memoir will appear. It will be the autobiography that got away.

*John Woodcock* by
**Rupert Alexander**
**Commissioned by MCC, 2006**
Perhaps cricket's most notable chronicler is John Woodcock *The Times* correspondent for over fifty years. Departing his cottage in Hampshire, occupied by only three Woodcocks since 1814, he covered fourteen tours to Australia.

Pre-match security
checks in the Media Centre
(David Gower at right)
Photographed by
Graham Morris, 2009

## A Writer's View
Angus Fraser

From the outside the Media Centre at Lord's looks like a spaceship hovering over the Nursery End of the Ground. When you emerge into it from the lift, it feels like that too. Yes, you have a wonderful view of the Pavilion and the game taking place, but you do feel slightly detached from everything that is going on. On major match days the Media Centre is in a world of its own, and some may say the utterances and written words that emerge from it are precisely that too.

It is easy to judge the state of a game by the atmosphere in the Media Centre. If the game is tight and at a pivotal point there is an air of quiet concentration and deliberation. If the match is going through a predictable and rather meaningless period there is chatter and laughter. If a big story breaks there is suddenly a lot of activity with private conversations and telephone calls taking place in quiet corners.

Most days follow a similar pattern, in that there is a relaxed feel before tea. After 4pm it gets serious as each writer finds out how many words to write and begins to construct his article, which needs to be ready for a 6.30 or 7pm deadline. Around this time the guests of the corporate boxes situated at either end of the Media Centre begin to get noisy. Loud, somewhat boisterous conversations are often interrupted by Derek Pringle of the *Daily Telegraph* shouting: "Will you lot shut up? There are people trying to work in here."

# 8.
# L'heure du Thé

As a specialist at Christie's, I had the pleasure of visiting some wonderful houses to compile inventories of some astonishing collections. I specifically recall visiting a flat high above Green Park, and tucked into a corner by a favourite desk was the painting illustrated on the previous pages. I was entranced by the scene, recognising it immediately as Lord's but curious to know why the crowd had tipped out onto the outfield. Of course now I know it as "perambulation", a time-honoured tradition of cricket intervals and, as I have read, a seemingly instinctive ritual of walking clockwise around the square.

Shortly after I joined MCC, this painting arrived at Lord's, a final bequest of Sir John Paul Getty. This particular scene was painted by the society artist Jacques-Émile Blanche. Having spent part of his childhood in London, he formed an attachment that never wavered and caused him to spend a part of each year resident at the Hyde Park Hotel to carry out his English commissions. The picture is entitled *L'heure du Thé* and captures an image of Lord's at one of the peaks

Previous pages: *L'heure du Thé* by Jacques-Émile Blanche (c.1928) was bequeathed to MCC by John Paul Getty Jnr, 2003. The fashionable spectators at the Eton and Harrow match perambulate on the outfield during the tea interval.

**Famous English Cricketers:**
**illustration from *The Boy's Own Paper* (1880)**
**Acquired by MCC,**
**date unknown**

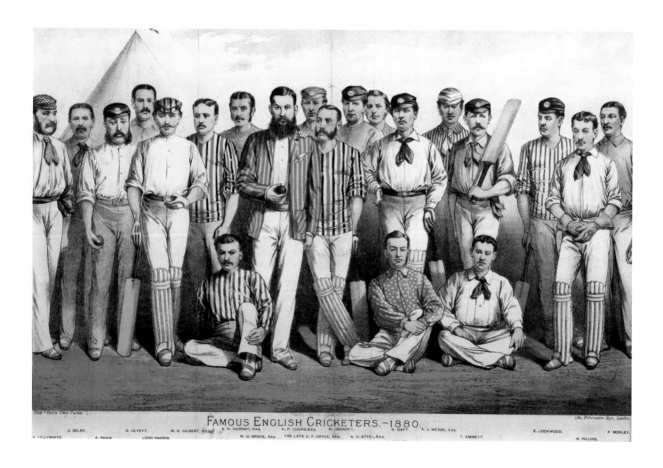

of its popularity. It can be dated to around 1928, just after the completion of the (then) new Grandstand by Sir Herbert Baker, but before the installation of his Father Time weathervane shortly afterwards. Judging by the dress of the gentlemen it is clearly the perennial public school derby between Eton and Harrow, the height of fashion at the time, when over 20,000 spectators would materialise on each of the two days.

The cream of society would dine on carriages, in luncheon rooms and arbours, and Blanche's loose brushwork wonderfully conveys the only moment that this ribbon of spectators unravels, onto the outfield, literally "flapping" in the breeze. There is no sign of the cricketers but that is just the point. It is the reason why in 1877, as the Wimbledon Championships were launched for the first time (with several cricketers among the entrants, including the winner), the finals match was delayed until after this weekend of cricket at Lord's.

A similarly wonderful image, though on a different scale, hangs in the Long Room courtesy of the Andrew Brownsword Art Foundation, which bought it at auction when sold by Kent CCC. It depicts the championship match at Canterbury of 1906 and is the work of Albert Chevallier Tayler (see p. 254), perhaps the most instinctive cricket artist of his time. Working from photographs often taken at Lord's, he also created a series of individual portraits for *The Empire's Cricketers*, published by the Fine Art Society in 1905, that illustrate not only a striking series of action poses but also the very texture of their cricket.

For players of the Edwardian Golden Age, classic cricket whites were *de rigueur*. This uniform tone lent emphasis to the cotton and flannel, wool and silk, cane and buckskin of their get-up. This emphasis on texture stretches back to the earliest days of cricket when, despite the coloured waistcoats, the on-field scene was likely dominated by black and white. Initially japanned shoes and silk stockings, silk jackets and velvet caps, nankeen breeches, followed by white dimity edged with blue, "duck" trousers, swanskin, flannel or white jean jackets, silk neckcloths, lace trim.

The painted and literary descriptions are happily borne out by the earliest extant cricket costume (c.1821), available to view at Lord's. Donated by the great-great grandson of the original player, Henry Daw, its veracity is confirmed by an exquisite miniature complete with cricket bat. In addition to the tight-fitting jacket, waistcoat and trousers, the sitter is portrayed with a blue scarf that picks up the fine blue stripes of the waistcoat.

This coloured trim, initially used by nobles to uniform their sides, was taken up by the professionals of the mid-century and employed to opposite effect. Players distinguished themselves with striped and spotted, or even zebra- and

leopard-patterned shirts, and when the Aboriginal Australians toured in 1868 they were actually identified by the colours they wore (see p.136).

By the late 1880s the various colours worn by touring teams were limited to caps, blazers and belts, as seen in the wonderful panorama of Lord's by Ponsonby and Barrable (see detail, pp.20–1). Here the two teams are accented in the colours of Melbourne and Marylebone but their whites are immaculate against the green of the Lord's turf and the wonderfully rich tones of the spectators.

W.G. Grace figures as one of the batsmen in this picture and his social status as the cricketing superstar of his day was overwhelming. He had a preference for playing in a "sweater", as it was already called, and wearing "white … it certainly looks better and cooler than any other colour". Special attention, he thought, might be paid to a jacket's colour, as when matched with a cap it made a pleasing contrast with white trousers.

MCC commissioned a portrait of the great man from the Academician Archibald Stuart Wortley, paid for by subscription, and are lucky enough to have extant correspondence between sitter and artist. W.G. was most particular about his pose and appearance, including the clothes he would wear, and took great pains over his sittings.

The MCC colours had changed in the middle of the 1860s, in time for both this portrait and the first-ever football international between England and Scotland, in which Arnold Kirke-Smith had taken part. Wearing the team's white woollen jumper with an England crest, he donned his own "pill-box" brimless cap (see p.27) in MCC colours throughout the match. W.G. fashioned the close-fitting brimless cap that was to give way eventually to the prized Baggy Green of recent Australian teams. Headgear was never limited just to caps, as the dramatic straw

**Tapestry belt worn by W.G. Grace, made by Mrs Grace**
**Acquired by MCC from B.C. Ridley, 1953**
The belt, its buckle fashioned with the legend "Cricket Forever", was reputedly given by W.G. to J.H. Rawlings, from whom it was acquired by Mr Ridley.

hats of Bosanquet and Foster bear witness (p.214), and this diversity seems to have had its origins in the earliest games, from the three-cornered hats and jockey caps of the 1740s to the "topper" of the early 1800s:

> Sir, I was at Lord's in 1851 and 1852 … the captain wore a tall black hat, being I believe the last non-professional to do so. The professionals continued to wear the hat much longer … a sort of badge of the profession. (Letter to *The Times*, 16th August 1919)

Then came straw hats and the soft cap from the 1850s, as advocated in an excerpt from *Felix on the Bat*:

> I recommend a cap of chequered woollen: it is light and cool to the head, absorbs perspiration and … is not likely to blow off and hit the wicket.

Indeed one of cricket's Laws, introduced in 1798, refers specifically to hats, prohibiting their use to catch the ball.

A pair of W.G.'s boots has also survived, despite the good use made of them by subsequent owners. Writing to MCC to detail their history, the donor recalled them being gifted to him by his father, who had found them just right if he donned a pair of thick socks, but he himself found them too big for practical use and so offered them to MCC in 1939. In his Lord's portrait W.G. dons brown boots, the staple of the old pro until the end of the century, though younger men had already begun the change to "pipe-clayed" white ones, as described in Pelham Warner's *Lord's*. Boots had not always been the fashion, with shoes – and co-respondent shoes at that (p.32) – preferred, "soled with sparrow bills", as spikes were once described.

In 1952 Don Bradman donated a pair of his size fives to Lord's new Museum; the committee pondered long and hard about accepting them. It seems no one really treasured "kit". Legendary are the stories about the Don gardening in his blazer and Bill Woodfull painting the fence in his so as not to sully his clothes. Keith Miller's 1948 "baggy" was lent during one Sunday afternoon match and the grateful recipient

**"Violet B. Westbrook"**
**Donated to MCC by**
**Miss P.V. Searle, 1961**
Miss Searle was the daughter of Violet Westbrook, Captain of the Red Team, Original English Lady Cricketers, c.1890.

told to keep it. As with the professional, likewise with the amateur: Benny Green in his *Lord's Companion* quotes Alec Waugh's attachment to his blazer:

> I used it as a writing coat … finally it fell to pieces in the early 60s … It embarrassed me on the cricket field, but it was a good friend, the companion of many contented hours.

Many players were just left with the pocket badges that have the symbolism of the belt buckles of old. Belts had taken over from braces, not least because, like ill-fitting clothes, the latter risked distracting the umpire from a correct decision. Belts might be decorative in a pair of fitted trousers. Silk scarves in club colours worn at the waist became a statement, and likewise tapestry belts with initials or patterns. The buckles display a wealth of imagery (p.225), one fine example being W.G.'s own engraved with "Cricket Forever", and another, dug up in a Somerset back garden, a lion's head with bat in mouth and serpent with the ball. The legend reads, "Strength wields the bat, wisdom guides the ball".

**Garfield Sobers and Muhammad Ali, 1966**
This is from a famous series of shots that includes Ali taking tea on the visitors' balcony as well as practising his backswing and socialising with the players in the Dressing Rooms.

It was not just personal taste and fashion that caused the changes in cricket dress. W.G. may have favoured wool above all else, but Felix was quick to point out the playing advantages of dress tailored to equipment. Though padding was derided at an early stage, round-arm bowling and uneven pitches may in large part have been a catalyst for the widespread use of long trousers under which India rubber or horse-hair pads (of which MCC has an example) might be secreted. More energetic play and a professional attitude suggested cotton scarves over silk for their heat-conducting properties. Similar things are happening today, introduced from other sports. The latest England uniforms have at last done away with the staple cable-knit woollen jumper and, while shirts do not yet have the GPS tracker pockets and adherent strips of rugby jumpers, it can only be a matter of time.

Rivalling these technical changes is the creeping influence of the commercialisation of cricket. In the eighteenth century the young Thomas Hope, descended from an old Scottish family but Dutch by birth, made play of his cosmopolitan nature by being painted in fashionable Beau Brummel style, playing cricket while on his Grand Tour of Italy, by the Swiss French artist Jacques Sablet (p.222).

Today's player is just as cosmopolitan, but not by dint of his style. Almost unrecognisable on the pitch – either shielded by his equipment or sunglasses, he is swathed in the logos, numbers, colours and names of his international sponsors. As if this graffiti weren't enough, it is entirely likely that he may be fashionably tattooed – in one case stickered – or individually patterned with suncream.

It is an ephemeral mix, made to look more fleeting still by its contrast with the traditional pristine, slogan-free uniforms of the baseball sides, whose game is commercialised in all aspects but this. Moreover it suggests that the visual impression of cricket will continue to change apace.

However, it may just be that a traditional element is never quite etched out of cricket at its most contemporary. Even in India's IPL, whose social cachet matches that of Lord's at its popular best, many of the teams have surprisingly regal names: Rajasthan Royals, Kings XI Punjab, Royal Challengers Bangalore, Chennai Super Kings. So too in MCC's recent portrait triptych, painted to symbolise the great qualities of Indian cricket, Kapil Dev and Dilip Vengsarkar bear close visual comparison to their predecessors of the previous century, John Wisden and George Parr (see pp.224, 228–9).

# National Pride

Among a host of ever-changing logos, the crests of today's international sides may seem to be enduring symbols of national pride. Each, however, has had its own idiosyncratic metamorphosis. South Africa swapped the Springbok for the Protea at the close of apartheid; the West Indies' island emblem is fashioned only for cricket; India's logo harks back to the Star of India, an order of chivalry created in the time of Queen Victoria.

**MCC team to Australia, 1903–4: signed photograph by J. Gazard, Adelaide Donated to MCC by P.F. Warner, date unknown**
This was the first tour officially organised by MCC. The players were kitted out in uniform blazers for the first time.

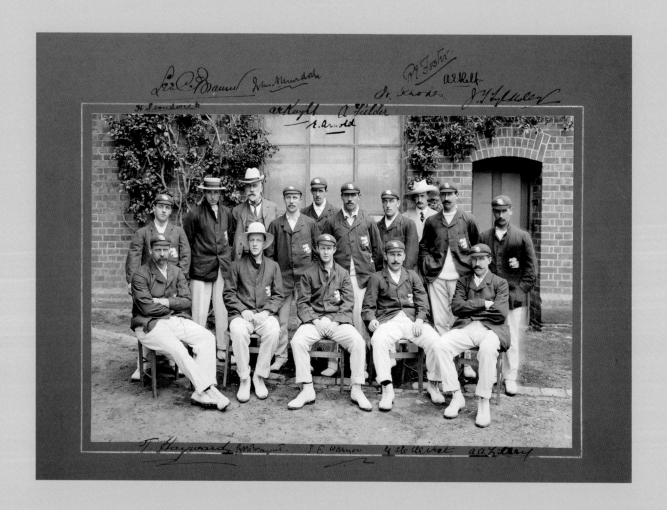

**Australian touring blazer
worn by Bert Oldfield, 1934
Donated to MCC by
Mrs W.A. Oldfield, 1976**
The old-fashioned crest
includes wirework and the
arms that are particular to the
Australian cricket team.

Pelham "Plum" Warner was celebrated at Lord's in the autumn of 2003 with the republication of his book *How We Recovered the Ashes* (prefaced by his granddaughter Marina). Scheduled to celebrate the centenary of the first MCC tour to Australia, its reappraisal was fascinating. Previous tours had been private business enterprises, but negotiations between the Marylebone and Melbourne Clubs – delayed by the outbreak of the Boer War – finally resulted in an authentic "England" touring side. It was not identified as an MCC side until some way into the tour, nor referred to as such by Warner in the book, and might never have been again had the side lost the rubber. The MCC name became preferred to that of England overseas for the next 70 years, and the George and Dragon arms were its emblem (see pp.128 and 251).

The history of the Australian cricket uniform is equally quirky. Prior to Federation in 1901, sides played in colours associated with their organisers or funders and so appeared in navy blue, black, red and yellow. However, with the formation of the Australasian Cricket Council (1892–9) and then the Board of Control in 1905, there was a conscious decision to fashion a uniform and crest or coat of arms. This represented Australian commercial endeavours of the time: wool-growing, shipping, mining and agriculture. A different national set of arms was fixed in 1912, but for reasons that remain unclear the cricket badges did not conform and to this day the device worn on the cap is particular to cricket.

**Tie! by JAK, watercolour cartoon produced for the Evening Standard (1975) Acquired by MCC, date unknown**

No one has better parodied the tie- and blazer-wearing MCC Members than Raymond Jackson, better known by his pen name JAK. Often his satire has lampooned them when they have been at their most entrenched, inevitably at a time of perceived threat. The debate over the dress code for the Pavilion at Lord's has always provided an opportunity for caricature and continues to do so – President Mike Brearley was the last to try metaphorically to ease open the Members' top buttons for match days. It was never better penned than in this cartoon of 1975.

**Ties from the Keith Williams Collection Purchased privately by MCC, 2011**

The idea of knotting a piece of cloth around the neck is close to 300 years old, so it seems the tie, like cricket, came into fashion in the eighteenth century. The Pavilion dress code continues to reinforce the Club's commitment to the collar and tie, though fashions change. Thirty years ago it was *de rigueur* not to wear an MCC tie at Lord's but presently one cannot move for the "egg and bacon". A recent innovation to the "City"-style tie introduced numerals to denote years of Club membership; over 1800 were sold in a matter of weeks.

" TIE ! "

**A Decorated ceramic patch box by Bilston (c.1776) Acquired by MCC from Timothy Millett Ltd, 2009**

Patch boxes held artificial beauty spots which were fashionable cosmetics in the eighteenth century. They came in a variety of shapes and sizes, were made of silk or velvet and known as "mouches". This particular example is transfer-printed, a technique developed in the 1750s. Although a step on the road to mass marketing, it was still a relatively expensive process and some hand-enamelling may have been involved in the production of this piece. It is one of the earliest souvenirs relating to cricket.

**Miss Wicket and Miss Trigger, a hand-coloured mezzotint after the picture by John Collet, published by Carrington-Bowles (1778) Donated to MCC as part of the A.L. Ford Collection by his nephew Hugh R. Ford, 1930**

This engraving was included as part of a series of pictures by Collet on "Ladies' Recreations". The others included foxhunting, shooting, skating and one entitled *Miss Tippapin*, for which several of the original pictures still survive. Miss Wicket is fitted out in a lady cricketer's costume with a fashionable bonnet but is shown striking a masculine cross-legged pose. The Countess of Derby was a player of note at this time, renowned too as the lover of the 3rd Duke of Dorset who was one of the great patrons and players of early cricket.

Effeminacy

**Cricket costume worn by Henry Daw of Christchurch, c.1821**

**Donated to MCC by Captain G. Milford-Cottam, 1970**

This is thought to be the earliest extant cricket costume and is typical of team clothing of the time. Henry Daw came from Christchurch in Dorset and is pictured in these clothes in a contemporaneous miniature by A. Varres. White linen shirts and breeches with knee fasteners and stockings were *de rigueur* for eighteenth-century gentlemen, possibly accented by team colours such as the light blue of Hambledon or MCC. By the 1820s traditional white shirts and long trousers were worn at all levels of the game.

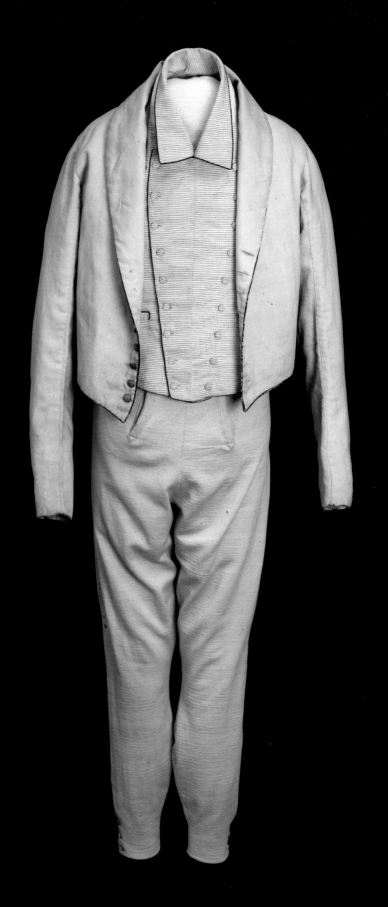

**A ceramic figurine by Mary Mitchell-Smith (1952) Acquired by MCC from the artist, 1953**

There is remarkably little information available about this sculptor who lived just over a stone's throw from Lord's at 150 Grove End Gardens. She is mentioned in passing by John Arlott in his account of cricket and art in *Barclays World of Cricket* (1980), and exhibited at the Arts and Crafts Exhibition Society in 1946 and regularly in the Royal Academy Summer Exhibitions between 1949 and 1970. This cricketer is nonetheless stylishly evocative and beautifully evinces the wonderful textures of his various "whites"; buckskin pads perhaps, light woollen jumper, cotton shirt freshly folded at the elbow, felt cap and supple gloves with just a hint of padding.

**Mr Hope of Amsterdam** by Jacques Sablet (1792) Acquired by MCC with the help of grants from the V&A Grant-in-Aid Fund and the NACF together with private subscriptions, 1968

This is perhaps the finest picture in the MCC collection and depicts one of the taste-makers of early nineteenth-century London. Thomas Hope's family were originally bankers in Amsterdam who amassed a significant art collection, much of which escaped with the family in the face of invading French revolutionaries. He continued to collect and settled at his house, The Deepdene, in Surrey. Here a 23-year-old Hope is pictured by a fashionable Swiss artist in Italy during his Grand Tour. The cricketing pose is strikingly unusual and surely points to his wish to be seen not only as decidedly English but also at the forefront of the vogue for cricket among the aristocrats of his day.

**Mansur Ali Khan of Pataudi in Brighton, 1961**

"Tiger" Pataudi had just turned twenty when this photograph was taken. Educated at Winchester school and Balliol College Oxford, he had inherited the title of Nawab of Pataudi from his father at the age of eleven. It was a momentous year for the young man: in July he was involved in a car crash that left him with permanent damage to one eye but, notwithstanding this, in December he was called up to the Indian Test team which won its first series against England, becoming captain the following year. In 1967 he married Sharmila Tagore, a ground-breaking star of Indian films, and they were one of India's most celebrated couples (see also p.152).

*George Parr, "Lion of the North"*, by William Bromley III (c.1850)
Acquired by MCC, 1895
"The ordinary dress of the day included a flannel jacket of short cut and a tall hat and I can say that the latter was no more uncomfortable than the billycock which succeeded it as headwear. Wisden was the first professional who wore a straw hat before the introduction of the cricket cap. They didn't mind a few stingers and they didn't wear India-rubber fingers. When leg pads were first introduced they were worn under the trousers, as though a hardy cricketer was ashamed of his cowardice in wearing them." Parr's dress, as described by Sir Spencer Ponsonby-Fane, seems to encompass attitudes both traditional and "modern" for its time.

**A jeweller's display pad of belt buckles (c.1865) Acquired by MCC, 2009**
These brass and gilt buckles with cricketing motifs in relief, such as cross bats and stumps, are displayed on a jeweller's pad with product codes handwritten beneath. Introduced in the 1850s, belts and sashes were early sought-after fashion accessories and soon became an important part of a cricketer's attire. These buckles would have been fitted to a canvas belt often printed with a cricket design. By 1868 belts were out of fashion and were replaced by elastic bands. However, belts and sashes in appropriate Club colours continued to be worn for scorecard identification.

**Cigarette case of
Jack Hobbs, 1930
Hip flask belonging to
Lord Hawke, 1897, loaned by
C. Ridley Esq., 2008
Match cases of H. Moss and
S.H. Pardon, 1890s, the latter
donated to MCC by Lt H.W.
Godfrey, 1968**

These objects are all reminders
of ages past when the idea
of smoking and drinking was
a part of sport just as much
as the playing. The cigarette

packets were actually found
under the floorboards of the
players' bathroom when the
Pavilion was refurbished
in 2004–5. They are also
testament to the long traditions
and etiquette of gift-giving.
The gold cigarette case,
presented by the Maharani
of Vizianagram, is engraved
"Dear Hobbs, Keep this as a
remembrance of your visit to
my house …"

**Bill Edrich and Jack Young,
photographed by
Fred Ramage, c.1948
Donated by Mr T. Young, 2009**

This photograph is a wonderful
evocation of dressing rooms
past. Bill Edrich, "Navy Cut"
in hand, examines what looks
like a silver tankard with his
Middlesex team-mate. Fred
Ramage was a legendary

Fleet Street photographer
who worked his way up to
be manager of the Keystone
agency. He was assigned to
the US Ninth Army during the
Second World War and stayed
on in Germany for two years
after it was over, photographing
the Nuremberg trials and
the first attempts to rebuild
Dresden.

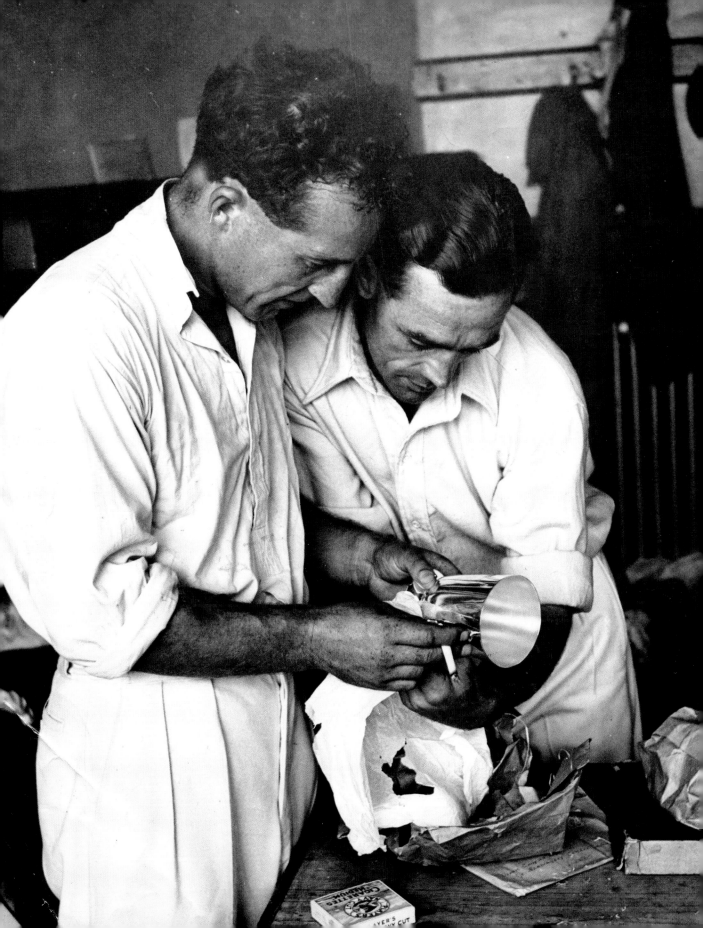

**John Wisden by William Bromley III (c.1850)**
**Acquired by MCC, 1895**
This portrait is one of four in the collections by Bromley, the others being of Jean-Émile Barré (the great real tennis player), George Parr and Alfred Mynn. Arguably the finest batsman and bowler in the country and leaders of the two rival All-England and United England XIs, Wisden and Parr are both definitively pictured at Lord's. Wisden was of course the founder of the Almanack, produced every year since 1864, and also instigated a sports goods company that sold equipment and apparel for a variety of sports.

**Kapil Dev by Stuart Pearson Wright**
**Commissioned by MCC, 2007–8**
This portrait was commissioned as part of a triptych to celebrate and represent Indian cricket at Lord's. Each figure embodied not only a tradition within India's game but had also performed wonderfully at Lord's. Dilip Vengsarkar, Bishen Bedi and Kapil Dev were the three chosen. The sittings took place at the Sir J.J. School of Art in Mumbai and the artist battled with 40-degree heat, intense public interest and hectic schedules. The landscape of the Brabourne stadium was laid in using flock, a quite inspired way to depict an outfield, and set up the almost hallucinatory figures. Retired from the game, Kapil was in the process of launching the ICL cricket league, intended to pre-empt the current IPL.

# A Style of Their Own

Wicketkeepers have often been thought of as a breed apart and England has a fine tradition of individual characters. They have encouraged caricature in a multitude of ways, from Godfrey Evans's mutton-chops to Alec Stewart's upturned collars, Bob Taylor's sweatbands to Paul Downton's sunhats. However it would be hard to surpass those two inveterate tea drinkers, Alan Knott and his protegé – Jack Russell.

Wicketkeeping equipment
of Alan Knott, Bob Taylor,
Jack Russell, Alec Stewart,
Chris Read, James Foster
and MS Dhoni
Photographed in the Home
Dressing Room, 2012
Donated, loaned and acquired,
1980s–2012

## Jack Russell's Mind Games

Russell is famous for reusing a single tea-bag – hung on his changing-room peg – for as many as twenty cups of tea. His lunchtime Weetabix covered in honey "had to be soaked for a minimum of twelve minutes in cold milk because I didn't like it too crunchy … I wanted it soggy so I could eat it quick and get it down."

His trademark black gloves, the tools of his trade, were entrusted to only one man to repair and repair and repair. This not only gave him a "feel for the ball" but added an extra dimension in his mind games against the batsmen: "Smell him out, Jack," or "Let him smell you." He adds: "It got a bit disgusting at various stages, but anything to get in the batsman's mind."

If the gloves were precious, his similarly patched-up hat was something of a fetish. "In the West Indies, they got me to change the head dress because it wasn't fitting with team policy … I had a bust-up with the management and it was either be sent home or wear official team hat … I got [it] in writing that I was allowed to cut this hat down. It looked no different to the hat I'd been wearing; in fact when we walked onto the field at Montego Bay Michael Atherton's heart jumped because … he thought I'd disobeyed him and put my old hat on … but I didn't, it was the new hat … after two games, it looked worse than my hat … so the whole point of the exercise – well, you'll have to talk to the powers that be, maybe they didn't like my individual eccentricities?"

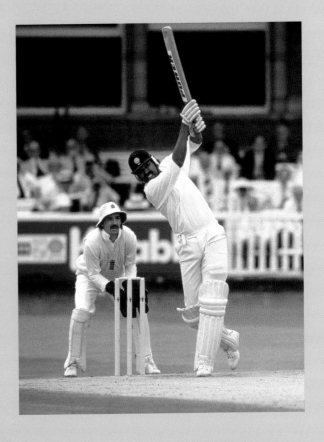

**Jack Russell and Kapil Dev, Lord's Test v India Photographed by Patrick Eagar, 30th July 1990**
Jack Russell keeps to the bowling of Eddie Hemmings, off whom Kapil scored four consecutive sixes to avoid the follow-on.

# 9.
# It's Not Just Cricket

Although by repute a traditional ground, and cricket its exclusive game, Lord's has a delightfully and surprisingly varied history. Whereas the autumn once presaged a long and gentle hibernation, the Ground's position in the heart of London and the commercial demands of a modern business now guarantee a wealth of visitors from all around the world throughout the year.

The museum's 2010 exhibition, partnering with the Baseball Hall of Fame in Cooperstown, New York to survey the connections between baseball and cricket, alerted many Americans to Lord's, but transatlantic links go back a long way. A work by one of the USA's most famous painters hangs in the Long Room and pictures two of the signatories of the American Declaration of Independence (see pp.12–13). The Museum's memorial inscription is taken from the American poet Russell Lowell, ambassador to Britain, who numbered Queen Victoria among his admirers, Henry James among his friends and was godfather to Virginia Woolf. Honorary members of the Club have included Dwight Eisenhower and more recently John Paul Getty.

One of the exhibition's images pictured a famous baseball match at Lord's (see below). This baseball tour was organised in 1874 by Harry Wright, whose father Sam had played cricket for Nottinghamshire. He himself played cricket for the New York Club of St George, and baseball for the original Knickerbocker side and went on to manage the original Boston Red Sox side. He had been keen to bring

*Base-ball in England: The Match on Lord's Cricket Ground between the Red Stockings and the Athletics* Coloured wood engraving from a sketch by Abner Crossman, *Harper's Weekly*, New York, 5th September 1874. Courtesy of National Baseball Hall of Fame and Museum

Advertisement for a Saturday evening entertainment at Lord's, 1867
Acquired by MCC, date unknown

baseball back to his "mother country" and arrangements were made through the efforts of another familiar name, Albert Spalding of the sporting goods empire.

The press whipped up interest in the tour, the first from overseas since the Aboriginal cricket tour, and promoted it as an American cricket tour which would play some exhibition baseball matches. The Americans had expected a little more emphasis on the baseball, but nevertheless agreed to play at both. Beth Hise related the events at Lord's in her masterly catalogue *Swinging Away: How Baseball and Cricket Connect*. On the first day of the cricket match, the Americans played an entire nine-inning exhibition baseball game during an extended lunch interval. Consequently they flagged during the afternoon, but were revived by a dinner for 50 gentlemen hosted by MCC's President that evening. The match resumed the next day, and after a weather delay the US side scraped ahead by a first-innings lead of two runs before rain washed out further play. The match was well reported in *Bell's Life* and *Wisden*.

In Georgian times the somewhat unreliable attraction of balloon ascents was launched. The huge scrapbooks of A.L. Ford contain original reports of Monsieur Garnerin's attempts in 1802 from Lord's in Dorset Square, and two previously unpublished watercolours tell of Mr Graham's efforts from the current spot in 1839 (see p. 57).

In 1844, for one week only a party of Native Americans – the first to encamp in Europe – perfectly replicated their "forest life" in a "romantic and beautiful scene" at Lord's. Their ball-playing, archery and dancing was something to behold.

Such catholic on-field entertainment has not survived, though musical ritual

**Lancaster bomber over Lord's, England v Australia, 6th September 2009 Photographed by Jim Dooley. Signed by air crew, donated to MCC**
This flyover was part of the celebrations for the 65th anniversary of the opening of the aircrew reception centre at Lord's.

has continued in one form or another. Don Wilson, coach to the Young Cricketers, was mentioned in *The Times* in 1983:

> The indoor school was brought to a halt by a sudden burst of beautiful choral singing. Those familiar with Don Wilson's eccentricities may have carried on playing, but others dropped their bats and listened. He had been coaching the boys of the Westminster Abbey choir school, and at the end of their net asked them to sing. He always does.

Neville Cardus, recalling his unalloyed joy of a quiet morning's cricket, noted:

> That's the proper way to enjoy Lord's: choose a match of no importance, for preference one for which the fixture card promises "a band if possible" … Lord's of all places should always have a band.

Music happily is now a staple of the international calendar, and the intervals' entertainments are extended to the Nursery Ground where the crowd has heard everything from pop bands to steel pans.

The march of military feet has echoed from the Ground's earliest gatherings, and Lord's has served as a mustering point for countless military parades, some formal, some less so: Bank of England and East India militia, wounded veterans arriving home from the Crimea, Yeomanry regiments on their way out to the Boer War (p.245), volunteers of the West Middlesex and Marylebone regiments attending their armoury, Americans and Canadians in the First World War, Royal Air Force recruits collecting for onward posting during the Second.

Jack Fingleton, feisty Australian cricketer and journalist, had a favourite story about Lord's:

> … one of two strangers in the Long Room watching a match … and ignoring the other – until a workman sauntered in, covered the bust of Dr Grace and carried it off. "My God," said one member to the other. "That can only mean one thing. That means war."

Cricket continued, of course, during the war and famous photographs attest to the near miss of a doodle-bug and the damage sustained by Father Time at the mercy of an errant barrage balloon. Some might argue that no finer cricket has taken place than that of the Victory Test Matches which marked the beginning of a golden period: Keith Miller in his pomp launching one of many sixes high into the broadcasting box above the England Dressing Room, Wally Hammond with a sensational flourish driving through the doors of the Long Room on his way to a hundred in each innings, and Learie Constantine captaining the Dominions to victory and fielding brilliantly.

Underlying the various military transformations, though, were a kaleidoscope of sporting activities. The armoury of the Middlesex Volunteers replaced a tool shed which in turn had replaced a skittle alley. From this same spot "Galloway" pony races started in the 1830s, galloping along a roadway as far as the east end of the Mound Stand (the old tennis court), north up the boundary with the Nursery Ground, and behind the Grandstand and Pavilion, completing a circuit of around 680 yards. This roadway also served as an athletics track along which running, jumping and even hopping competitions took place.

William Slatter recalls the wet days of the 1840s and 1850s:

> Games of all types were played by the members in the Club room – even that of marbles … Boxing competitions also took place … and I have heard my father say that he often got more tips on a wet day, doing a little boxing, than on many fine days.

Billiard tables were not only available in the Tavern, but also as a particular feature of the Members' rooms built above the new real tennis court in 1838: "two of the best that can be manufactured, the one by Thurston, the other by Burroughs."

A bowling green was installed at the Pavilion End, and James Dark rented land near the North Gate from Henderson's Nursery for archery. Prior to 1896, lawn tennis was played on the match Ground when there was not an MCC match taking place. Five or six courts were in use on Saturday afternoons and Dick Gaby acted as the tennis marker. The real tennis pros were all useful cricketers and used to turn out often for the staff cricket club, known in its early days as the St John's Wood Ramblers. George Lambert, champion tennis player, was reputed to be as hard a hitter on the leg side as the great George Parr. At least they were the only two that could be remembered clearing the tennis court roof without taking a slate.

Real tennis had been introduced to boost a flagging membership and succeeded in its aims (p.242). Since that time the tennis membership has always thrived and today is busier than ever. A European Championship is held annually and the Tennis and Rackets Association chose to hold their centenary dinner at Lord's in 2008. This popularity did not stop the court's demolition to make way for new stands in the early 1900s, but did mean that it was rebuilt using its old floor and preserving its famous "bounce" for generations to come. The Club boasts arguably the finest library on the sport and two of its oldest pictures are on a tennis theme.

**Men's Lacrosse Team, Nursery Ground, c.1905**
**Acquired by MCC, date unknown**

Committee minutes note the preparation of the Nursery Ground for lacrosse in 1903, but the Sport & General Picture Agency archive was destroyed in the Blitz and so no accurate identification has yet been made.

That donated by the Dowager Duchess of Mayo pictures pallone, another game once (and only once) played at Lord's (p.243).

Experimentation with alternative sports has not ceased in recent times. Slatter does not recall lacrosse in his career, although it is recorded as early as 1876 and a Canadian women's team was perhaps the last to play in 1953. Varsity hockey matches took place on the outfield in the 1970s and the Ground saw a dramatic defeat of India by Pakistan in a pre-Olympic hockey tournament in 1967. The Nursery Ground narrowly avoided the installation of a golf range in 1963 but did succumb to a dry ski-slope in the late 1970s. And, on a winter theme, a temporary ice-rink was very nearly installed three years ago.

This entrepreneurship continues without threat to the playing surfaces, through what used to be the off season at Lord's: the huge International Wine Challenge, design and art shows and banqueting for all occasions. Lord's is a filming location too – and a destination every year for over 60,000 tourists who do not come to see the cricket but to savour the atmosphere of its history and traditions.

# Slings and Arrows

Thomas Lord advertised his first ground as available to archers in 1788, the year after it was founded, and archers frequented the Violet Hill area of St John's Wood in the latter part of the eighteenth century. Founded in 1781, the Toxophilite Society gained royal patronage in 1787 and in 1832 settled its headquarters at "Archers' Hall" in Regent's Park. Around the same time James Dark rented land to set up butts, yet it took another 175 years for the greatest-ever gathering of archers in London to congregate at Lord's.

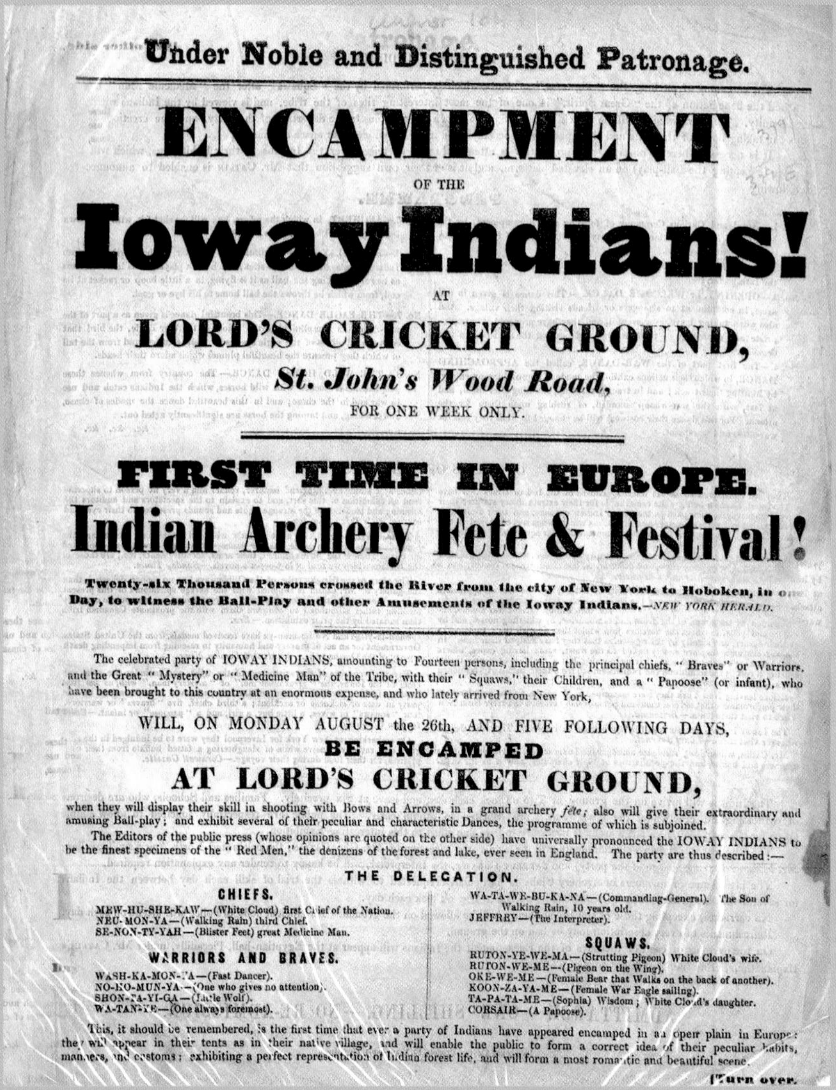

Advertisement for the
Ioway Indian Encampment
at Lord's, 1844
Courtesy of the Roger Mann
Collection

**British Archery Team at Lord's, Photographed by David Klein, 2007**
The British archers hosted a number of trial events in the run-up to the 2012 Olympics including triangular series with India and China

The qualifying rounds of the 2012 Olympic tournament began on the Nursery Ground, with competitors shooting towards the trees in St John's Wood Churchyard from a line of small tented pavilions, as picturesque as those described in George Eliot's *Daniel Deronda*. In the wooded glade of the Coronation Gardens, the stout defensive stroke of W.G. Grace's over-lifesize statue looked insufficient defence against the attempts of novice archers aiming at four targets beside him.

The famous nineteenth-century Pavilion on the other hand had received the 21st-century treatment: the Secretary's Office had been given over to the anti-doping agency, the bar turned into the "Protocol Office"; in the Long Room the famous pictures of Bradman and Miller, Jardine and Hutton surveyed a series of purple and pink fittings complete with Coca-Cola vending machines. It seemed to match more aptly than ever the postmodern Media Centre,

which itself was bedecked for the fortnight with Olympic rings.

Out on the pitch the excitement of 5,000 spectators in steeply banked rows of seats ebbed and flowed on either side of the competitors. Often this was in time to the short, sharp bursts of music that accompanied not only winning arrows but also moments of suspense and tension. In between times the knowledgeable American commentator could be heard stringing together the action, while high on the upper balcony *Test Match Special*'s Jonathan Agnew was doing the same for his radio audience. He enthused in spite of the erratic weather: "Archery doesn't normally attract much of a crowd so to compete in a place like this, with the huge stands right on top of them, must [have felt] very special for the competitors … The Italians winning the gold medal in the team event was one of the most dramatic things I've seen in sport and I didn't expect archery to do that for me. It's ruthless …"

**Rob Fahey** by
**Rupert Alexander**
**Commissioned by MCC, 2011**
The Tasmanian Rob Fahey has proved the greatest player the world of real tennis has ever seen. In 2006 he equalled the record for World Championship singles defences, held by the legendary Frenchman Pierre Etchebaster, and has since won three more consecutive titles. Real tennis has been a feature of Lord's since a court was first built in 1838. The artist was delighted by the challenge of portraying Rob on court at Lord's and the painting was chosen as part of the National Portrait Gallery's touring exhibition in 2012–13.

**Pallone at Naples** by **Pietro Fabris (c.1768, detail) Bequeathed by Geraldine, Dowager Countess of Mayo, 1944**
Pietro Fabris is not a well-documented artist but the quality of his work is undisputed. His best-known pictures are those for Sir William Hamilton, the famous geologist and diplomat (ambassador to the court of Naples), whose collections of antiquities were bought by the British Museum and Thomas Hope (see p.222). It is a wonderful coincidence that *pallone* itself was once played at Lord's. A.L. Fisher recalls his attempt in 1852–3 to stage a game by encouraging the plethora of London-based Italian refugees. Though successful, it proved a one-off event.

**RAF Commemorative Plaque on the Pavilion Wall Unveiled by Air Chief Marshal Sir Peter Harding, 1992**

The Chief of Air Staff was invited to memorialise the use of Lord's as the RAF's No.1 Air Crew reception centre in the Second World War: 115,000 civilians and 44,000 military personnel passed through the doors between 1941 and 1944. They shared the Ground with 903 Squadron Balloon Barrage, part of London's defences against low-flying enemy aircraft. On the 65th anniversary in 2009, surviving members returned to Lord's; an exhibition of Guy Gibson's "Dambusters" squadron complemented a fly-past by an original Lancaster bomber (see p.236).

MANY ENTERING THE RAF THROUGH GATE No 1 AIR CREW RECEPTION AREA AT LORD'S DURING THE SECOND WORLD WAR GAVE THEIR LIVES. OUR ENJOYMENT OF CRICKET REFLECTS THEIR SACRIFICES

**Berkshire Yeomanry Volunteers at Lord's, photographed by Russell & Sons, 1900**
**Donated to MCC, before 1907**
Originally formed as mounted cavalry in 1794 during the Napoleonic wars, the Volunteers are here pictured before heading to South Africa for the Second Boer War. They were continuing the traditions of Lord's as a mustering point for the army that began with the Bank of England and East India Volunteers in the 1700s. At one stage the Middlesex Volunteers actually based their armoury on site.

THEIR·HIGH-HEARTED

**Henry Allingham and bust of W.G. Grace**
**The bust donated to MCC by Mrs Grace, 1919**
**Photographed by Clare Skinner, 2007**
Henry Allingham received publicity in 2007 when he was recognised by Guinness World Records as the oldest living British man and later the longest-lived veteran of the British Armed Forces. Born in 1896, he recalled seeing volunteers returning from the Second Boer War and watching W.G. Grace play cricket before he served at the Battle of Jutland in 1917. Although a Londoner, he had never visited Lord's, and his request to do so was swiftly granted. He is pictured here in the Museum.

**World War II Memorial Board, Lord's Pavilion (detail)**
**Commissioned by MCC, 2004–5**
The MCC Museum was originally established as the Imperial Cricket Memorial Gallery, dedicated to all cricketers who lost their lives in conflict. Its memorial plaque, with words from the American poet James Russell Lowell, is complemented by two ornate boards hanging over the staircases in the Pavilion that record the names of Club Members who died in the two world wars. At least two of these were awarded the highest medal for gallantry, the Victoria Cross: Brigadier General Edmund Phipps-Hornby and Captain Francis Grenfell.

**Drawing for a treatment of the Lord's Hotel Signed by W.H. Slatter, August 1917**

It was reported that the destruction of the Club's wine cellars was the great loss of the fire of 1825. There can likewise be no doubt of the importance that Thomas Lord attached to supplying wine to MCC, situating his shop at the entrance to the Ground.

The construction of a new hotel in 1867, with money forwarded by William Nicholson (of gin fame – see p.112), was enthusiastically received and soon became a well loved feature and entrance to Lord's. It was a measure of this that the decision to demolish it caused such hand-wringing within the membership exactly one hundred years after it had been created.

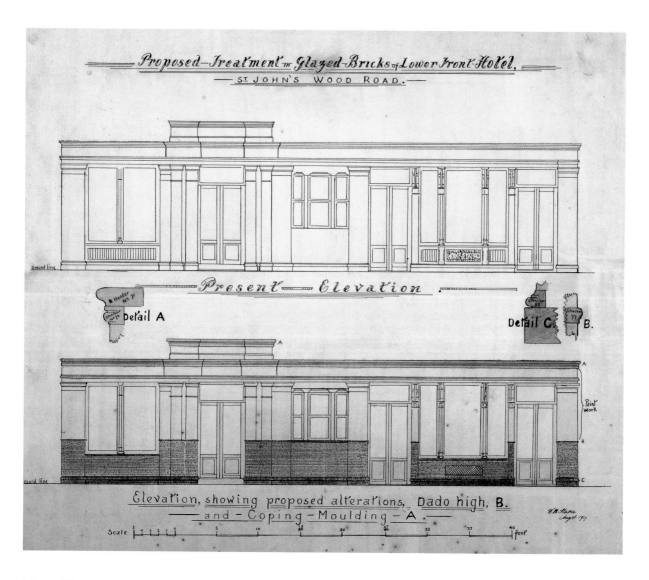

**Pen and ink drawing, copy from *The Bystander* (1903)**
**By W.H. Slatter, 1904**

Pelham "Plum" Warner is here pictured surprising Australia when his pie is opened. Culinary analogies are commonplace in the art and literature surrounding cricket, a game whose rhythm is marked by time and food. George Portman was the master caterer at Lord's for almost 50 years, running the Lord's Hotel and match-day hospitality during the season and an off-site catering business during the winter. Queues ran down St John's Wood Road to the back of the Mound Stand where his bakery sold MCC-monogrammed chocolates. These he supplied from underground rooms dedicated to chocolate, marzipan and other confectionery, and he was renowned, even during the war years, for being able to supply whatever spectators or MCC required. At the height of his career he earned more than the Club Secretary, was always seen in his Daimler and when his health failed was sent to Menton on the Riviera to recuperate.

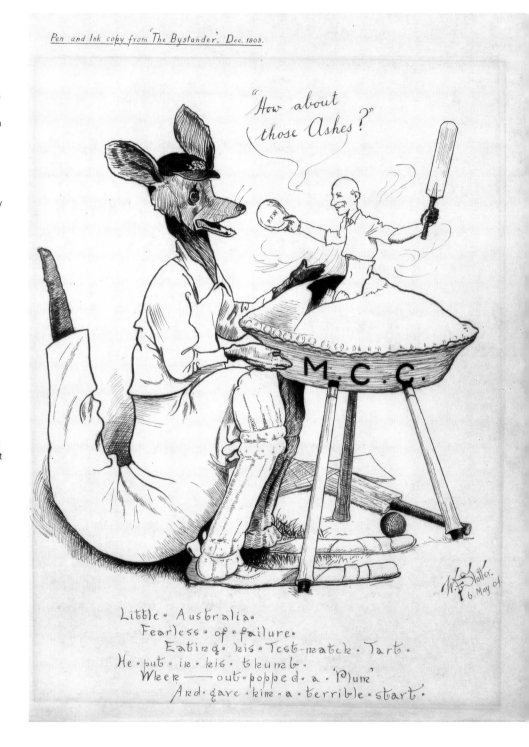

**Sir Horatio Mann by Hugh Douglas Hamilton (c.1785) Loaned to MCC by Lord Cornwallis, 1947**

Nephew of his namesake, the British Resident in Florence, and successor to his Baronetcy, Horace Mann was one of the great patrons of cricket in the eighteenth century. His activities can be traced through *Scores and Biographies* (see p.172) and his friendships with 3rd Duke of Dorset and Horace Walpole, the great correspondent. He hosted matches at all of the estates he owned during his life and eventually was a victim of his own hospitality, bankrupting himself by his involvement.

**Size 2 salmon flies of
Colin Cowdrey
Donated to MCC by
G. Harman (?), 1988**
Member of the House of Lords,
past President of MCC and the
Lord's Taverners, and England
captain, Colin Cowdrey is
still described as the perfect
gentleman. His quiet sense
of fun was as evident on the
pitch as off, whether in the heat
of competition or relaxing at
the racecourse or on the river.
No doubt the description of
his masterful cover drive – "a
final persuasion of the wrists"
– might equally have been
applied to his casting.

**Portrait of Sir Donald Bradman
by Robert Hannaford (1972)
Donated to MCC by the
Commercial Bank of Australia,
photographed by Clare Skinner**
Bradman's portrait, by one
of the finest living Australian
artists, is here pictured
alongside a portrait of one of
his great friends, R.W.V. Robins,
during filming of the famous
BBC *Antiques Roadshow* series
which has twice been held at
Lord's. On this occasion it was
produced in association with
Sport Relief to raise money for
charity.

**Poster advertising London
Gardens Exhibition, 1960s
Acquired by MCC, 2008**
Cricket has always been
inextricably linked to gardens,
ever since its beginnings in
eighteenth-century London.
The White Conduit Club played
next to the pleasure gardens in
Islington, and at Dorset Square
the first Lord's Ground was

close to not only Marylebone
Gardens but also Flora Tea.
The Nursery Ground (see p.73)
operated as a market garden
and Mr Henderson, who ran
it, was renowned for his tulip
shows. During the Second
World War it was returned to
cultivation as allotments for
the war effort.

RED-LETTER DAYS
FOR GARDEN LOVERS!
SEPTEMBER 6, 7 & 8
COME TO THE
LONDON GARDENS
EXHIBITION
ORGANISED BY THE LONDON
GARDENS GUILD AND THE
"DAILY EXPRESS"
AT
LORD'S
CRICKET GROUND
Classes open to all amateurs. Schedules on application to 9, Gower Street, W.C.1. Music each afternoon. 6,000 sq. ft. of flowers. Garden advice free.
THE GREATEST AMATEUR
SHOW EVER HELD
ADMISSION 6d. ONLY
PROGRAMME FREE
HOW TO GET THERE
Buses: 2a, 2c, 2d, 13, 48, 53a, 74b, 279b
Underground: St. John's Wood Station

**Michael Vaughan and Natalie Lowe training for the BBC's *Strictly Come Dancing* TV series**
**Photographed in the Long Room by Clare Skinner, 2012**

Michael Vaughan is the latest in a series of retired cricketers to have entered this competition. They have proved unsurprisingly adept at picking up the skills of ballroom dancing and the consequent publicity has raised the profile of cricket with whole new audiences. This visit is a reminder of a long and continuous tradition of celebrity visits to Lord's – Sir Edmund Hillary and Sherpa Tenzing in 1953, for example – and the range of filming and events held around the Ground throughout the year. At left can be seen Albert Chevallier Tayler's painting of the championship match at Canterbury (see p.209).

**Tibetan monks on the Lord's Tour, 2010**
**Photographed by Brian Thompson**

The Club's Museum opened in 1953 but it was not until 1990 that MCC considered running tours for members of the public on non-match days. Since then the numbers have risen to over 60,000 per year from all parts of the globe. Visitors have included ex-street gang teams from Los Angeles and architects from Scandinavia, as well as great players and their families keen to soak up the atmosphere behind the scenes.

# Stirling Stuff

Despite the Ground's total transformation since the 1830s, it seems the Club had no need for a professional architect until it sought to build the Pavilion in 1889. Thomas Verity and his son Frank then worked with the Club for twenty years. They were succeeded by Sir Herbert Baker who in turn maintained a 30-year association, beginning with the memorial gates to W.G. A half century later, a second transformation began.

J.P. Morgan Media Centre, 2008
Designed by Future Systems, built by Pendennis Shipyards and Centraalstaal BV, 1995–9

The impetus for the modern landscape of Lord's was galvanised by both Colin Stansfield-Smith, who persuaded the Club in 1979 to start a serious investment in the estate, and then Peter Bell, who introduced a series of architects whose innovatory commissions set Lord's apart.

The Mound Stand (1987) was the catalyst, embodying tradition and innovation simultaneously. The "pitch" from Hopkins Partners promoted the essential character of the Ground with an independent stand, canopied like the Pavilion, and built on the terraces and arches of Frank Verity's 1898 design. Yet its huge capacity was designed to float on only six columns roofed with Teflon and glass-fibre fabric. As James Offen (Estates Committee member) puts it: Hopkins, who had been neatly pigeon-holed as a high-tech architect, was accused by the critics as having "turned the clock back a century", yet MCC was praised for backing such a "daring design".

David Morley's Cricket Academy and Nicholas Grimshaw's Grandstand followed, culminating in the most individual piece of architecture since the Pavilion. Woefully inadequate conditions for the press were the driving force behind the J.P. Morgan Media Centre, designed by Future Systems, a wild card inclusion on the competition shortlist. Few of their designs had actually been realised and their scheme, when put to the Committee, was not preferred by President, Treasurer or Secretary. Costs soared beyond the original budget but its critical reception was emphatic: winner of the Stirling Prize for Architecture in 1999, and acclaimed as "One of this century's best buildings in Britain ... a triumph of both form and function ... a stunning vantage point".

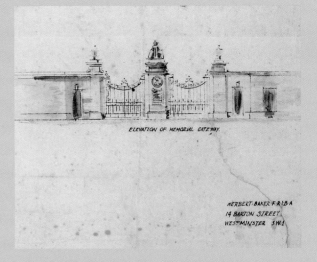

**Elevation of Grace Gate
Original watercolour by Sir
Herbert Baker (c.1919–23)**

ERECTED TO THE MEMORY OF
GEORGE ROBERT CANNING
1 LORD HARRIS 1932
BY THE M.C.C.
ECOGNITION OF INVALUABLE SERVICES
ERED TO CRICKET AND TO THE CLUB OVER
IOD OF MORE THAN FIFTY YEARS HE WAS
EAT CRICKETER A GREAT GENTLEMAN
AND A WISE COUNSELLOR WHOSE
HUSIASM FOR THE GAME NEVER WANED

10.
**Future Imperfect**

The collections at Lord's tell you nothing if not that cricket has been in a constant state of flux for its entire history. Lord's and MCC have for the majority of that time been at the centre of the cricket world and so either riding the crests or wallowing in the troughs of the waves. The Club was slow to react to the developments in bowling that saw the underarm become the overarm; it tiptoed around the issue of "shamateurism" – the payment of supposed amateurs – personified by W.G. Grace; it suffered through the diplomatic spat of the "Bodyline" affair, and fumbled the issue of cricket and apartheid that resulted in threats to damage Lord's own square. Yet it has also elicited respect, especially in latter years, for its guardianship of the Laws, its maintenance of the Ground and its unchallenged commitment to supporting and promoting cricket throughout the UK and in developing nations.

That such change still continues to affect the game today should give no cause for disquiet. However, current challenges seem to have even broader international scope and to move at a swifter pace than ever before. They concern not only traditional series but huge tournaments in at least three different formats of the game and a wealth of interested parties – sporting, political, commercial – in a range of nations. Given that MCC and Lord's are themselves subject to this change, what does the future hold?

Perhaps it would be illustrative to turn to the *Wisden* Almanack as an indicative comparator: a traditional, independent pillar of cricket's history and, bearing in mind its contributors, one of the most intelligent commentaries on the cricketing scene. As a book of the most traditional kind, it has not been immune from the vagaries of the publishing world. Sales have declined as the industry has been challenged by the capacity and speed of the internet. An annual almanack flies in the face of 24-hour news and ever-updated statistics and it has relied until recently on a benign owner to shield it from the increasingly harsh reality of business. New ownership has changed its outlook and, although an Australian edition did not extend beyond eight issues, the new *Wisden India Almanack* has just been launched with great fanfare and associated digital accompaniments in the shape of a website and quarterly supplement.

The familiar feel of *Wisden* has altered too. Its cover carries photographs, and its size fluctuates, reflecting a change in content that perhaps now lends more emphasis to comment than statistics. This may be the result of a series of different editors, who have come and gone contrary to the past tradition of the Almanack, or it may just be that it seems uncomfortable in its own skin. In 1997 Sanath Jayasuriya was nominated as a Cricketer of the Year even though he had not played at all during the English season; his "influence" on it stemmed from his

Previous pages: The Memorial Wall, Harris Garden. Photographed by Richard Green, 2012.

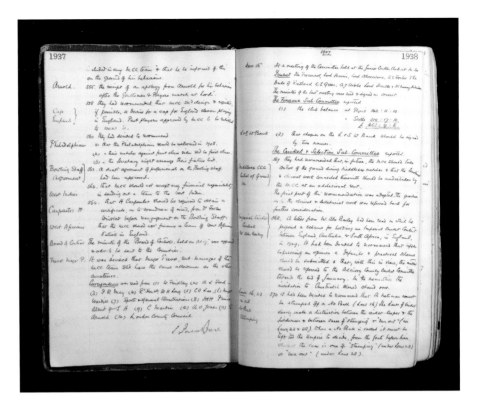

**MCC Minute Book, 1907**

At a meeting on 16th December an Imperial Cricket Contest was suggested. This led to the instigation of the Imperial Cricket Conference in 1909 that became the International Cricket Council in 1965.

performances in the 1996 World Cup. From 2000 to 2003, the award was based on cricket "round the world", before a new category – Leading Cricketer in the World – was inaugurated in 2004. Historically the *Wisden* roll of honour settled for a reflection of the state of the game in England, but this hesitation over its primary annual award would suggest that for today's game this is not enough. Yet in an increasingly digital world perhaps the Almanack's very particular physical characteristics stand for something. It is more than a list of figures, a set of blogs; it is the literary and statistical standard by which others are measured and it is a tactile and visual link to the traditions of the game.

MCC faces a similarly testing time. The cricketing forecast looks changeable, to say the least, with difficult economic conditions predicted for the foreseeable future and first-class cricket in England attracting catastrophically low attendances. Television rights shield the counties from the naked truth and MCC is in no position to alter radically the game's governance or to effect a swift generational shift in social attitudes to cricket.

That is not to say it does not still harbour ambitions in this respect. Handing over the reins to the ICC and ECB was not taken lightly, nor was control ceded quickly. In 1907 MCC responded to a request from South Africa for an international tournament by establishing a representative organising committee, the precursor of the ICC. Associate nations were subsequently added to the group, again by request, and it was only in 1964 at the suggestion of Pakistan that the new conference was established and the World Cup subsequently born. On the domestic front, MCC still retained a symbolic link, through its name and colours, with England's touring sides into the 1990s and control transferred slowly to the Cricket Council and then the Test and County Cricket Board in 1968 before the ECB was established in 1997.

MCC's currently declared position of neutrality with regard to control of the modern game has brought mixed blessings. It has certainly facilitated its ongoing guardianship of the Laws. The Club's long tradition in this role, a matter of record within the archive at Lord's, justifies this delegation and brings a sense of continuity for the future. It shields the ICC from accusations of partiality or unnecessary modification, although a whole new series of playing conditions, dictated by the ICC, give a somewhat contradictory elasticity to the application of the Laws.

This assumed impartiality has allowed the development of MCC's World Cricket Committee, an initiative to draw senior players, or those recently retired, into a constructive and structured public debate about proposals for change to the betterment of cricket. Discussions on lie-detectors, four-day Test Matches and the Decision Review System give the Club a good profile and by ICC's own admission may have influence on their executive decisions.

The emphasis of MCC's activities has changed and continues to change from executive administration of cricket to promotion of playing and discussion of the game. This is underlined by its advancement of the Spirit of Cricket campaign which seeks to encourage fair play and is directed at everything from the Indian Premier League to the Chance to Shine campaign reintroducing cricket into schools.

What then of Lord's? How have these changes affected people's perspective of the Ground? As home to a variety of cricket authorities, not as much has changed as might have been expected. ICC only left in 2005 after 96 years at the Ground, citing government intransigence over tax breaks, and conferences still occur on

**Bound telegrams of MCC Tours to Australia 1928, 1932, 1936**
**Donated to MCC by The Exchange Telegraph Company's Service, 1977**
These books record the historic communications between England and Australia during the infamous "Bodyline" controversy.

a regular basis. ECB remain despite the sometimes frosty relationship that has existed with its host and its development of the national centre of excellence at Loughborough. MCC's "impartiality" in cricketing affairs (and reluctance from county members) is said to prevent a closer relationship with Middlesex than has existed to this point. So despite MCC's reduced role, the governing bodies of cricket retain strong ties with Lord's and in doing so present a diverse profile at the Ground.

Lord's of course still owes much to the Members who own it in the best traditions of Club membership; a tradition, incidentally, to which so many football clubs presently hark back. They are the reason the name of its founder – Lord – remains, unburdened by advertising, synonymous with cricket. Although they cannot hold back the advancing commercial tide, they provide a cautionary check, enabling Lord's to be partnered with the most apt commercial sponsors. At the

*Lord's in Danger: The MCC Go Out to Meet the Enemy* (1890) **Pen and ink cartoon donated to MCC by 1907**
MCC succeeded in heading off the threat of development by the railway company, but only just.

LORD'S IN DANGER.   THE M. C. C. GO OUT TO MEET THE ENEMY.

[" Sir EDWARD WATKIN proposes to construct a Railway passing through Lord's Cricket Ground."]

same time they encourage its identity to be forged through preservation of its finest historic features – be they buildings or spaces – coupled with the development of new architecture that often acts as a model for other sports grounds around the world.

The tone of this architectural development has certainly been focused on cricket as its main attraction. The stands have been renewed separately, retaining their own identities, refuting the notion that Lord's is a stadium, an amphitheatre. The outfield has been removed to enable new drainage but, in spite of this significant work, has not been levelled. The gardens and Nursery Ground have been retained and not developed, all in the tradition of Lord's as a cricket ground. Sticking to these principles has however limited the extent to which Lord's can be commercially developed and seemingly prevents its adaptation to a more diverse set of events, as was once the case; no grass court tennis tournament, no MLB baseball games, no outdoor concerts. Why should that be of concern? Ironically because it is cricket that presents a threat to the current site.

There is no doubt there is more cricket played than ever before at Lord's. Two more wickets have been added to the square in the last twelve months to

*Ashes...*
**Cartoon by Peter Brookes for *The Times* (2005)**
A reinvention of the Ashes urn with a meaning in direct contrast to its original connotations of the Ashes of victory.

accommodate demands for the continuation of historic fixtures such as Eton and Harrow and Army and Navy, as well as the regular international and first-class games. However there remain questions over the long-term future of Test cricket and Lord's has been given only short-term guarantees for staging international matches and first-class finals. A chicken-and-egg situation has developed in which future guarantees will not be forthcoming unless development is made; yet how can development be justified without the guarantees? Grounds around the country have at the same time increased the level of competition by developing in the knowledge that they can diversify the use of their stadia in a variety of ways seemingly not open to Lord's.

Given the diminishing responsibilities of MCC, the development of its main asset has assumed ever larger importance and the development plans of the last ten years have caused heated discussion for good reason. It has missed several opportunities in the past to secure its future and risks doing so again. Fortunately it may be that the deadlock is easing. It seems that the Club's wider contribution to cricket, such as its funding of university teams throughout the UK and its rather better known work with Sri Lanka's Foundation for Goodness in the wake of the South Asian tsunami, may play a more significant part in the conditions of its bid for that elusive longer-term staging agreement.

The collections too will play their part in this, promoting the facilities at Lord's, helping to contextualise the Ground's more modern features and to bring Lord's past to light for visitors today. There are not many places in which people have gathered continuously to play or enjoy sport for over 200 years. Though it may not bear the UNESCO trappings of a World Heritage site such as Kew Gardens, it certainly shares its characteristics. A destination for visitors from all over the world, it showcases the finest matches one can see but at the same time nurtures and promotes the understanding and playing of cricket. It celebrates the diversity of the game but is cognisant of and honest about the problems and threats that face it; never more so than on one Sunday morning in 2010 when the influence of bookmakers and illegal gambling surfaced during the Lord's Test. Whether it is hosting "home" matches for the "homeless" Pakistan side, testing technology in the Academy, or researching coloured balls or the Laws via the collections, Lord's should remain an example for others to follow – and a home to cricket.

# Reputation

It would surprise many that Lord's might be considered as Yorkshireman Hedley Verity's home ground (he played more Tests here than at any other venue). It's equally surprising to think of it as Ian Botham's natural habitat but perhaps unfairly so, for this would be the consequence of a single incident, the culmination of Kim Hughes's tactic of keeping Botham "in his box and let[ting] the press do the rest". It was at Lord's that Botham bagged his only pair, returned to the Pavilion amid pained silence from MCC Members, and resigned the captaincy of England.

**Sir Ian Botham and Andrew Flintoff Photographed by Andrew Weekes, 2007**
The reception following the investiture ceremony for Ian Botham's knighthood was held in the Long Room here at Lord's.

Ian Botham, Lord's Test v
Australia, 7th July 1981
Photographed by
Patrick Eagar
Ian Botham returns to the
Pavilion after a duck, which was
to result in his resignation as
England captain.

Ian Botham debuted at Lord's in June 1978 as a *Wisden* Cricketer of the Year. He was only 22 but he hit 108 and took eight wickets in an innings against Pakistan, a feat still unmatched by anyone, anywhere in the world. In his final eight overs and five balls he took six wickets for a paltry eight runs. In August he returned to take match figures of 11–140 and ran out Richard Hadlee into the bargain. By the end of his career he had taken five wickets or more at Lord's against every Test-playing nation of the time, including 8–103 against arguably the finest West Indian side to appear at "headquarters".

When the nadir of his career occurred in 1981, Mike Brearley took over the captaincy. Brearley was not exactly the archetypal MCC man, but many still thought him the antithesis of Botham, yet it was their relationship that rekindled the fabulous form that had deserted the great all-rounder. In Brearley's own words: "He and I got on well, if at times turbulently.

He was excellent for me and not only in the obvious ways – taking wickets, scoring hundreds, and catching brilliantly at second slip. He also made me feel younger, made me laugh, kept me on my toes. He would tease me, bring me down to earth, so there was something symmetrical in our interaction, as well as the more obvious asymmetry."

As the patrician atmosphere of Lord's has mellowed, perhaps the appreciation of Ian Botham's skills and attitude has grown further, given even greater emphasis by the sort of relationship that Brearley describes. There is too a fitting symmetry that, having learnt his first professional skills as an MCC Young Cricketer, he returned to Lord's to celebrate his knighthood.

**Sir Garfield Sobers by Sara Raphael**
**Commissioned by MCC, 1992**
Commissioned without demur in 1992 when the idea was first proposed, the portrait was a surprise to some at Lord's, though acclaimed by those in artistic circles. Painted from life, it captured the great cricketer at the end of his career (if not in his dotage) rather than in his pomp. Uncertainty seems to be the key element: the anticlimax of life outside the spotlight, the challenges of the ageing athlete and a future lacking financial security.

**Glenn McGrath by Justin Mortimer**
**Commissioned by MCC, 2010**
This painting has a melancholic mood, although McGrath retired from Tests with great plaudits after a 5–0 series whitewash of England in 2006–7. He was a consummately metronomic fast bowler who took full advantage of the Lord's slope and took his 500th Test wicket here (see p.127). The uncertain futures of both Test cricket and the truly great fast bowlers are tied together: shorter formats favour shorter, faster spells that reward and preserve the fast bowler far better than back-to-back Tests.

**More Expert Opinions on the Lord's Wicket** by Roy Ullyett
**Acquired by MCC, date unknown**

This cartoon lampoons the unevenness of the wicket at Lord's, a comment not only on the obvious slope from north to south but also on the infamous ridge at one end of the central square that caused consternation in the 1960s. Generations of groundsmen and technological advances have ironed out problems both with the pitch and outfield, but the adherence to tradition and reluctance to level the Ground has limited future possibilities for other sporting or non-sporting events.

**Play Up, Play Up …: Stone frieze by Gilbert Bayes (1934) Commissioned by MCC through the generosity of David Isaacs**

The creation of this bas-relief was part of a lengthy and not altogether satisfactory negotiation between MCC and the local council to build new arbours along the perimeter of Lord's. Dedicated to St Marylebone, it depicts a curious collection of sports bound together by the famous line from *Vitaï Lampada* by Henry Newbolt. In retrospect it reflects the history of Lord's as a multi-sports venue and Victorian amateur values, but seems incongruous with its future as exclusively a cricket ground with a strong commercial ethos.

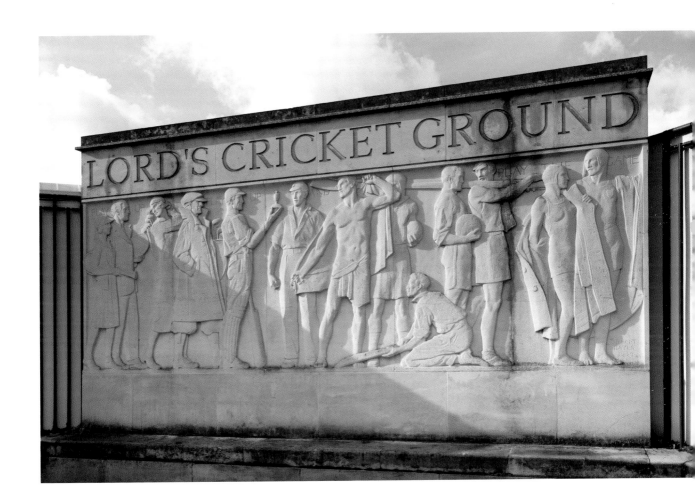

**Mohammed Yousuf celebrates a century at Lord's Photographed by Graham Morris, 2006**

Mohammed Yousuf, known previously as Yousuf Youhana, is one of the greatest in the long line of talented Pakistani batsmen. He holds the record for an innings at Lord's for his country (202), but sadly at the time of writing the Pakistan side are unable to play international cricket in their own country on account of the political situation. Although the intention is to return as swiftly as possible, there is no telling when this will be.

***Inzamam-ul-Haq* by
Brendan Kelly
Commissioned by MCC, 2006**
Inzamam is a controversial
figure in England for an incident
that occurred when he was
captain of his side in 2006
(his side forfeited a match
at The Oval after a protest in
response to accusations of
ball-tampering). It has tended
to overshadow his reputation
in this country and mask a
true appreciation of his batting
prowess. MCC commissioned
this picture during that tour
and although the sittings did in
fact take place its completion
and unveiling was necessarily
delayed.

**Victorian Enamelware
Photographed by
Peter Dazeley, 2012**
In the last twenty years Lord's
has become very much an
architectural village. Its
buildings – and some of the
specific techniques it took
to make them – span almost
the 200 years during which
cricket has been played on
the Ground. The ingenuity and
skill of the Victorians not only
resulted in the Grade II*-listed
Pavilion (built in a mere twelve
months) but also the finest and
most efficient enamelware ever
to be installed at Lord's.

**J.P. Morgan Media Centre**
**Photographed by**
**Peter Dazeley, 2012**
The commission for the Media Centre went to a firm that was added to the shortlist of competitors as a late "wild card". It was first and foremost a concept, the construction of which was only finally resolved using the skills of boat builders Pendennis on the south coast in unprecedented fashion. It has changed the face of Lord's, now rivals the Pavilion in its familiarity to international visitors and – like the new Mound Stand – has spawned a host of imitators from the West Indies to India.

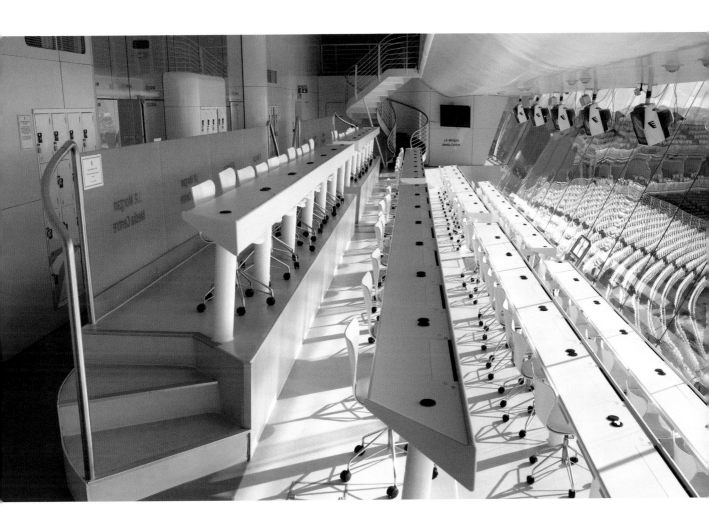

**MCC cricket uniforms
1930s–1980s
Donated or loaned to MCC**

MCC organised its first official tour in 1903–4 and England continued to be known as MCC on tour right up to 1977. Even after that, England touring teams retained the colours of the Club, and it was only in 1997 that this ended. The nature of touring has changed almost beyond recognition, and with the impetus of the IPL touring may well be giving way to not only limited-over but also Test championships.

**World Series Cricket
"Australia" uniforms, 1977–8
Acquired by MCC as part of
the Barratt Collection, 2013**

This revolutionary series of international matches over two seasons was the product of a commercial battle for television rights to international cricket in Australia. It completely changed the face of cricket for a short time, transforming the match-day scene with advertising, colour, floodlights and of course money. In doing so it set a precedent for the Indian Premier League, which once again challenges the accepted rhythm of the English county season and international tours to the UK.

**Test, One-Day and Indoor
Cricket balls
Manufactured by Duke & Son
and Kookaburra, 2008–9**
The development of coloured
cricket balls has been
pioneered by MCC at Lord's
in partnership with Imperial
College London in efforts to
respond to the challenges of
day/night cricket. The goal is to
find a ball that retains its colour
and hence its clarity in spite
of the wear it suffers on more
abrasive pitches. The incentive
comes from the popularity of
the limited-overs format and
the notion that bigger crowds
will come after dark.

**MCC team v Champion County Sussex, 2007 Photographed by Polly Hancock in the Harris Garden, Lord's**

The tradition of the season-opening match between MCC and the winners of the previous year's County Championship stretches back to 1970. During the 1950s and 1960s Surrey and Yorkshire, more often than not the Champions, had come to Lord's. Pictured here in MCC's 2007 team are: (standing) Zoheb Sharif, Tim Bresnan, Alex Gidman, Graham Onions, Nick Compton, Alex Loudon, Steven Davies and Adil Rashid, and (seated) Owais Shah, Matthew Hoggard, Alastair Cook (captain) and Steve Harmison. For the last two years the match has been transferred to Dubai, testing the new coloured balls under lights.

**Scoresheet for England v Pakistan, Fourth Test at Lord's, 2010**
**Compiled and donated by David Kendix**

The atmosphere at Lord's during this Test Match changed from one of euphoria to incomprehension. Jonathan Trott and Stuart Broad scored a record partnership of 332, but the scoresheet is more notable perhaps for the No balls bowled by Mohammed Amir and Mohammed Asif. Match-fixing and the pressure on players to arrange certain aspects of a game is an ominous and creeping presence in today's game.

| MATCH BETWEEN | ENGLAND and PAKISTAN | | COMPETITION 4th Test | | DATE 26 August 2010 |
|---|---|---|---|---|---|
| PLAYED AT | Lord's | | ON 26, 27, 28 August | | |
| UMPIRES | B F Bowden & A L Hill ; TV: S J Davis | | SIDE WINNING TOSS Pakistan | | ELECTING TO Field |
| | Referee : R S Madugalle | Scores: D Kendix & P J W Danks | | | |

| ORDER | Time IN | Time OUT | Time for 50/100 | Time for 150/200 | BATSMEN | RUNS AS SCORED | MINUTES/BALLS | HOW OUT | BOWLER | Totals |
|---|---|---|---|---|---|---|---|---|---|---|
| 1 | 140 | 234 | | | * A. J. Strauss | 12313111 // | M 54 / B 37 | bowled | M Asif | 13 |
| 2 | 140 | 1101 | | | A. N. Cook | 141211 // | M 64 / B 37 | c K. Akmal | M Amir | 10 |
| 3 | 235 | 149 | 90/154, 155/194 | 203/431, 274 | I. J. L. Trott | 41344411211211141414412211412141111443411351241211111143111311111111122111412214141411111 // | M 557 / B 383 | c K. Akmal | W Riaz | 184 |
| 4 | 1102 | 1108 | | | K. P. Pietersen | // | M 6 / B 1 | c K. Akmal | M Amir | 0 |
| 5 | 1109 | 1114 | | | P. D. Collingwood | // | M 5 / B 3 | lbw | M Amir | 0 |
| 6 | 1115 | 1122 | | | E. J. G. Morgan | // | M 7 / B 3 | c Y Hameed | M Amir | 0 |
| 7 | 1123 | 149 | | | + M. J. Prior | 14123241111 // | M 106 / B 72 | c K. Akmal | M Amir | 22 |
| 8 | 150 | 153 | | | G. P. Swann | // | M 3 / B 2 | c A Ali | M Amir | 0 |
| 9 | 154 | 1244 | 108/165, 124 | 773/348 | S. C. J. Broad | 142124111112122211124612142411414414411242122111311431111241111141111411114444111 // | M 390 / B 299 | lbw | S Ajmal | 169 |
| 10 | 1245 | 143 | | | J. M. Anderson | 24 // | M 18 / B 14 | c Y Hameed | S Ajmal | 6 |
| 11 | 144 | 149 | | | S. T. Finn | | M 5 / B 1 | not out | | 0 |

| RUNS | MINS | OVER | RUNS | MINS | OVER | RUNS | MINS | OVER | 332 PARTNERSHIP for 8th wicket | Bonus Points: B 4 | | 4 |
|---|---|---|---|---|---|---|---|---|---|---|---|---|
| 50 | 106 balls | | 200 | 432 | | 350 | 694 | | - Test match record | Batting: L 11212114112 | | 17 |
| 100 | 232 | | 250 | 494 | | 400 | 773 | | | Bowling: W 511 | | 7 |
| 150 | 328 | | 300 | 562 | | 450 | | | | NB 14 | | 14 |

| | 1 | 2 | 3 | 4 | 5 | 6 | 7 | 8 | 9 | 10 | PEN | |
|---|---|---|---|---|---|---|---|---|---|---|---|---|
| FALL OF WICKETS | 31 | 39 | 39 | 39 | 47 | 102 | 102 | 434 | 446 | 446 | TOTAL | 446 |
| BATSMAN OUT | 1 | 2 | 4 | 5 | 6 | 7 | 8 | 9 | 10 | 3 | | |
| OVER | 11.1 | 12.6 | 14.1 | 14.4 | 16.1 | 38.2 | 38.4 | 134.2 | 138.5 | 139.2 | FOR 10 WICKETS | |
| NOT OUT / SCORE | 10 | 8 | 8 | 8 | 16 | 45 | 45 | 180 | 184 | 0 | OVERS 139.2 TIME 612 | |

**Yorkshire jumper of Brian Close and Lancashire blazer of Cyril Washbrook Acquired by MCC in 2012 and 2010**
The Lancashire red rose and familiar Yorkshire colours conjure memories of two England greats, giants of the first-class game and *Wisden* Cricketers of the Year. Whereas taking part in a Roses match once meant as much as representing England, their counties' traditional rivalry is however on the wane. The popularity of new Twenty20 teams, falling championship attendances and the closing of many smaller county grounds have led to calls for drastic changes in the county structure.

# State of the Pitch

In 2012 Mick Hunt, Head Groundsman at Lord's, his team and their turf consultants replaced over a third of the outfield and prepared the pitch to perfection for a Test Match between the top two sides in the world less than a fortnight after the London Olympics archery competition. Not only that, but they also added two further tracks to the main square in response to the ferocious demand for cricket at Lord's. Mick, who started at Lord's in 1969, was most recently named Groundsman of the Year 2012.

**Mick Hunt, Lord's Head Groundsman Photographed by Graham Morris, 2009**
Starting with Steevey Slatter, the groundsmen at Lord's have been David Jordan, Percy Pearce, Thomas Hearne, Harry White, Austin Martin, Ted Swannell and Jim Fairbrother. Mick is the longest serving of all.

***Triptych of Lord's*** **by Jonathan Warrender (detail)**
**Commissioned by MCC, 1995**
The artist developed a speciality for the detailed "bird's eye view", which he first honed painting rural estates and has subsequently adapted to golf links.

## The Groundsman's View

Mick Hunt

I started as a junior and worked up the ladder. We always promote in-house because unless you know the quirks, like the slope of the pitch and the sheer number of matches, it would be *shock, horror!* The slope is a nightmare. If I could change one thing about Lord's I'd like a nice, level square … but when you've got an eight foot six inch drop from one side to the other, you'd probably have to dig up half of Lancashire to backfill it!

Once there's frost, that's a no-go, keep off. It freezes the water in the leaf of the grass so it acts like an icicle. If you walk on it, you break it. Snow too, but snow's actually quite good for grass so long as it doesn't lay too long.

There's only really a two- or three-week period when there's nothing you can do outside, but the season starts earlier and earlier. We used to start the pre-season rolling in March – now we're starting in February.

From April to the first week of October we work seven days a week and ten, eleven, twelve-hour days. The grass is mown three times a week. The grass should look nice and green but I've purposely starved it to get the roots to go down – if we get a hosepipe ban I want the root structure there.

But conditions have to be right. Those are the pitches for the whole season. You get it wrong and it's wrong for the whole season. There's no point rushing it. I spend a lot of time looking at the sky!

# Acknowledgements

# Picture Credits

After almost a decade at Lord's, I nevertheless feel as though I am still batting through a morning session. Solid foundations have been laid for the innings to come, but the character of the side has yet to be fully revealed. I have relied to this point upon a terrific team of staff, some permanent, some temporary, who have thrown themselves into their work and achieved a huge amount in a relatively short space of time. I hope they have taken just as much from the experience as I have.

We are fortunate to enjoy an excellent relationship with the Arts and Library Committee members, both past and present, who have through the Chairmen, Robert Fellowes and Alastair Lack, provided great enthusiasm and wise counsel in turns. Additionally there has been a great range of individuals and organisations with whom we have forged partnerships, created exhibitions, published books and research, acquired wonderful items for the collections and shared Lord's and its history. It has been a real pleasure and an experience that I hope will only continue to grow.

My thanks go to all of those mentioned above and of course to my parents, who first fostered my passion for cricket and art.

*Adam Chadwick*

All images courtesy of Marylebone Cricket Club except as follows:

pages 1, 8, 12, 15–17, 29, 30, 33, 35–45, 51–54, 58, 61–5, 67–70, 72–3, 78–81, 84–7, 89–96, 98–100, 105, 107, 109, 111–17, 119, 122–5, 130–7, 139–140, 142–4, 146–151, 153–6, 158, 161, 164, 166–174, 176–7, 179–187, 189–198, 200–03, 206–7, 211, 214–15, 217, 219, 221, 225–6, 230, 235, 239, 244–5, 247–9, 251, 253, 257–263, 270, 276, 277, 280, 281: Richard Green
2–3, 47, 59: Philip Brown
4: Courtesy of the National Football Museum and Sports Heritage Network
6, 48–9, 56, 60, 76–7, 88, 128–9, 145, 152, 162, 205, 272, 282: Graham Morris
11, 28, 32, 50, 82, 118, 138, 157, 208, 210, 216, 222, 224, 228, 243, 250, 268, 283: © Marylebone Cricket Club, London, UK / Bridgeman Art Library
10, 120–1: Richard Buckland
14, 101, 126, 246, 252, 254: Clare Skinner
20–1, 34, 46, 141, 165, 175, 204, 218, 220, 229, 242, 269, 273, 278: Richard Valencia

22: Private Collection
24: Courtesy of Christie's Images / Bridgeman Art Library
25: Priory Collection
27: Tate
31: Courtesy of Bonham's
57: British Museum
66, 102–3: Matt Bright
71, 75, 97, 199, 231, 267: Patrick Eagar / Getty Images
74: Sarah Williams
110, 152: Tom Shaw / Getty Images
127: Anthony Devlin
163, 178: Patrick Eagar
188: Clive Mason / Getty Images
212, 239: Sport & General Collection / Press Association
223: Getty Images
227: Keystone Picture Agency
232–3, 271, 274, 275: Peter Dazeley
234: Courtesy of Milo Stewart Jr./ National Baseball Hall of Fame and Museum, Cooperstown, NY
236: Jim Dooley
240: Courtesy of the Roger Mann Collection
241: David Klein
255: Brian Thompson
256: David Hares
266: Andrew Weekes
279: Polly Hancock

# Index